THE ARTS
OF THE
CHURCH

RICHARD H. RITTER

THE PILGRIM PRESS
BOSTON

Copyright 1947

THE PILGRIM PRESS

PRINTED IN THE UNITED STATES OF AMERICA

To

My Wife

A Worshiper in Spirit and in Truth

Preface

The primary object of this book is to induce study of the church arts. Individual readers, study groups, committees on music, drama, or worship, and college and theological students are invited to read and debate its propositions. The author does not mean to intimate that the way he prefers to worship is the only correct way; even his own local church does not worship in just that way. He has joined in a great variety of expressions of worship, not only with all the main types of Christian denominations, but with non-Christian religions in a score of countries. He has never engaged upon such a fellowship with sincerely religious people without having been drawn into the spirit and the glory and the power of it. He was ordained by Presbyterians, has shared in the ministry of Congregational, Baptist, and Methodist churches, and an interdenominational college chapel, and acknowledges his profound debt to the Russian Orthodox Church in whose services he joined regularly for over a year.

Recently there has been much thinking and some writing about the relations of art to worship and the Church. There is still much to be done, not only by liturgists, artists, critics, and historians but also by the men and women in the pews of our churches.

In a sense this book is not the author's at all. It has grown out of a group called the Congregational-Christian Arts Guild, which has appointed him to do the work and which has greatly stimulated his thinking. He has been aided by the advice and suggestions of the Master Craftsmen of the Guild—particularly Von Ogden Vogt, Clarence Ward, C. Harold Einecke, Fred Eastman, and Albert E. Bailey; by officers of the Guild—Harold G. Jones, John R. Scotford, Charles A. Butts, John B. Hanna, and Alfred Paul Focht; and by other members—Douglas Horton, Mrs. Einecke, Pierre DuPont Vuilleumier, Mrs. Chester B. Fisk, Bliss Wiant, Tertius van Dyke,

and particularly Mrs. Ritter. Mrs. H. C. Camp has assisted with
the typing. However, the author alone is responsible for the general philosophy as well as for the detailed opinions set forth.

The Arts Guild is a movement more than it is an association.
Though it cannot avoid controversial issues, it seeks never to act
the pontiff. All of us are coming more and more to see that by the
carefully planned use of many arts our common worship can be
made more powerful and more significant than it has generally
been. Thinking of ways to further this purpose is worthy of the
busiest layman's as well as the most successful minister's earnest
effort. Indeed much of the final success or failure of Christianity
will depend upon how well Christians understand and practice
the arts of worship. Art is more than a mere adjunct to life. It is
more than a handmaid to the Church. It is more than tinsel or
decoration. It is something fundamental, built into the very stuff
of our religion. When its art is poor, it is probably because Christianity itself has been weak, effeminate. When its art is great, it
can be taken as a sure sign that there is a strength within which
demands strong modes of expression.

Contents

Illustrations

The Arts of the Church

CHAPTER I

Where Art Begins

What Is Art?

LET US ASSUME at the beginning that there are three great elements in every work of art: an object outside of the artist which is sensed or perceived; a relationship of some sort between that object and the artist; and an outward response to his perception on the part of the artist.

Although each of these three elements is important, since there could be no art without them all, it is the last of the three in which we are particularly interested when we seek to define art. For objects in the world are constant no matter how they are perceived; and the personal relationships between an artist and his object are so individual and complex that no outsider can fully understand or define them. The third element—the response of the artist to his object, or to his perception of the object—produces the work of art itself. Art, then, is perception, relationship, and reaction; but its most interesting and significant aspect is reaction.

All of us are artists. For all of us perceive; all of us enter into some kind of relationship to that which we perceive; and all of us tend to express to some extent at least our reactions to our experiences and relationships. Furthermore all of us make our expressions in different ways. No two people would describe a house, a view, a cow, a person, an event, God, in just the same manner. Therefore we all are creative.

A certain teacher of history, seeking one day to demonstrate to his class how unreliable are the stories of even eyewitnesses to historical happenings, strode grumpily into his room, stamped around, lost his temper, shouted out strange and wild commands to his pupils, and finally, apparently losing all control of himself, knocked one of the boys down. Having quieted the excitement, the teacher then laughingly explained that it was merely an experiment, and asked the pupils to write down the story of exactly what he had said and done. There were thirty pupils and there were thirty accounts; and they differed widely in practically every detail. The teacher's point had been made.

Again, there was an art exhibit in the Brooklyn Museum not long ago, consisting of a hundred portraits of Abram Walkowitz by one hundred different artists. And how amazingly unlike they turned out to be! All of us show some reaction to the experiences that come our way: the people we meet, the books we read, the events we witness, the beauties we see or hear. Yet each does it in his own way. Each paints a picture of something which he has seen, so to speak, through his own colored glasses; and he does his painting, perforce, with the materials and by means of the talents which are at his own disposal. Sometimes we seek to convince a person that we are the only ones who have seen a certain object correctly. We know that it was brown not gray. We insist that every reasonable person accept brown, reject gray. This however is not art but propaganda. It is dogmatism; for every man has a right to his own reaction.

Some may think that art is the literal reproduction on canvas, or by means of a musical instrument, of what we have seen or heard in nature. Aside from the fact that it is impossible really to make a reproduction in another medium, what good would this do? One might better go look at or listen to the original. Copying has its uses, as in advertising, illustrating, or science, but it can hardly be called art. Art is creative. It appeals to the imagination. It is the setting forth in meaningful form of the innermost thoughts and emotions, brought into being by a confrontation with some external object. True art does not seek to convince or convert; nor is it a search for beauty. Art is expression for its own sake, expression for the satisfaction that expression gives. And all of us, unless we are perverted by one means or another, crave such expression. To that extent we are all artists.

There are many ways of expressing one's self. Words provide the most common media, ranging in significance from scolding and swearing on up through descriptions, stories, poetry, and drama. The effect of words can be strong, beautiful, and vibrant, or it can be harsh and ugly. Most of us have not learned how to use words to their full effect, but to what extent we do, to that extent we are artists.

Pantomime is another medium that we all use. We gesture; we shrug our shoulders; we smile; we frown; we grimace; we give a cold or haughty stare; we cast coy glances or raise our eyebrows in scorn or curiosity. Certainly this is an expression; and it is also the beginning of one of the great arts—drama.

Most of us enjoy music. Our varying moods call for songs, jolly or sad, or for hymns, or for "swing." Or we "compose" a tune of our own, humming a melody that was never heard before in all human history and never will be heard again. Perhaps we have learned to write down little symbols on five-lined staffs in a way which can be translated into sounds by those who know what the symbols mean. Or, lacking the ability to compose, we sit down at the piano and play, if we can, one of Chopin's preludes, Beethoven's sonatas, or Irving Berlin's ditties as a means of expressing our mood.

The clothing that we wear, the houses in which we live, our furniture and the way we arrange it, the pictures we hang on our walls, our lawns and gardens and hedges, our choice and arrangement of books or flowers, our method of throwing a baseball, our cooking: all of these express to anyone who cares to notice something of what is within our souls. Here, too, is the beginning of art.

Painting, carving, modeling, lettering, sewing, embroidering, dancing, acting:—one could fill pages just enumerating the arts. And the instruments, or tools, which we have devised to assist us to give form to these arts are truly amazing in their diversity. Think of the number of musical instruments, the variety of the wood-carver's tools, or the kinds of thread that one may buy, and we begin to see how extensive is art and how intricate are its ramifications.

Art, then, if this definition is correct, is any significant expression of what takes place within us when we are confronted by an outer object. Whether the art be good or bad depends not only on how beautiful or meaningful is the object, but even more on how rich is the personality of the artist and how skillfully the artist uses his medium. Even though the experience be profound, if the expression is petty the art is bad. Without some profundity of experience, on the other hand, it would be difficult if not impossible to produce good art. Many a profound thought is left badly expressed and even undeveloped because the author of it is not a great personality, or because he has not disciplined himself in the techniques of his art. Whenever that happens it is a pity; all of us have the responsibility both to live at our best and to try to give significant expression to that best.

No one of us is complete in his artistry. Each of us, even after a lifetime of effort, is still largely unexpressed. Even Michelangelo, master painter, sculptor, architect, and competent poet, has not left us all we would like to know about his soul. As long as we are even partially unknown to anyone who wishes to know us, we must strive to be artists. This is our bounden duty and it is for the most part a pleasant one.

What Is Christian Art?

IT IS AS EASY to define Christian art as it is to define Christianity, for Christian art is the expression of Christianity. We must recall that it is not beauty that we are striving for in art, but an honest, earnest expression of our thoughts, emotions, imaginations, and ideals. If our Christianity is a deep, real thing, then our art will become the same. A vigorous Christianity will demand to be vigorously expressed, just as a sentimental Christianity will be satisfied to be expressed sentimentally. We can safely leave beauty to shift for itself. If our souls are beautiful, our purposes intelligent, and our art honestly expressed, then beauty will surely appear.

Let us, then, seek not to express our Christianity beautifully but rather to express it honestly and skillfully in whatever media we use.

When I say "Christianity," I really mean, of course, "Christian experience." Christianity as an objective, historical fact is not something that we express. We perceive it, become aware of it, study it, understand it ever more and more, and come gradually to appreciate at least certain phases of it. It is not until we have come into some kind of contact with it and experienced it in our own lives that we can even begin to express it. To be a Christian artist, as Maritain has said, one must first be a Christian and then an artist.

There are people who will disagree with us here. Some will say that Christian art is the artistic representation of Christian objects. That is: any picture of Jesus would be Christian art; or any representation of a saint, or of a Biblical subject; or any poem which deals with a Christian or a Biblical theme; or any dramatic performance of a Biblical or ecclesiastical episode. Such a definition of Christian art seems quite inadequate. The mere fact that a scene is from the Bible does not necessarily make it Christian. A painting of the slaying of the Amelikites or of the incident of Ananias and Sapphira might, in fact, communicate un-Christian values. Again, is it not possible to present a Christian object in a non-Christian way? How many weak, priggish, effeminate representations of Jesus have passed themselves off as Christian art on the grounds that they were pictures of Jesus! On the other hand, how many handsome, glamorous, boy-scout-ish, football heroes on canvas have been named "Jesus" by their artists! Both of these extremes obviously exhibit a misunderstanding of Jesus. Some of the artists of the Renaissance, especially in Italy, used models for the Virgin who could hardly have been capable of bringing up a son to be a Jesus. One artist is even accused of having used a prostitute as a model for a Madonna for the sole reason that she was beautiful. Can such a picture be called Christian?

Then again there are other people who say that anything that is intended to produce, or that does actually produce, a Christian effect in its beholders is Christian art. By such a criterion, a dramatic play, for instance, that leads the audience to act like Christians, or a statue or piece of music which sends people forth to do such deeds as would delight the heart of Jesus, would be a Christian work of art. Now no one would deny that this contention is nearer to the truth than the former one; yet it is not an easy matter to state whether such a work is Christian or not. A church singer who has no spiritual motivation, but sings only for money, not caring whether he is paid by church or night club, can hardly be said to be a Christian artist. If the congregation, believing the singer to be sincere, is enabled to express its Christian feelings through the singer's song, the congregation may be acting in a Christian way. Yet, in the long run, insincerity in the artist will no doubt be found out, and the people will be unable to express their Christianity through his work. One would hesitate to call the work of a non-Christian artist Christian even though it might inspire Christian acts or give voice to the aspirations, thoughts, or emotions of sincere Christian people.

Unless one knows the inner feelings of an artist it might at times be very difficult to distinguish between Christian art and Jewish, Confucian, humanistic, or even atheistic art. This would be true in the realm of ethics also. Honesty and purity, as well as prayer and a sense of the presence of God, are ideals which are present in more religions than Christianity. It is enough that the artist himself should be convinced that what he is seeking to say is Christian. He need not despair if he is not well understood by men. If the world does understand, so much the better. But if not, at least he has been true to himself and has found the ease of spirit and the satisfaction and joy of fulfillment which are the prime rewards of any artist. In many cases, however, the testimony of a work of art is so clear that there can be no question at all as to its Christianity. The soul of the Christian artist shines through his production, and all beholders say with one accord, "Lo, the glory of God!"

This, then, for better or for worse, is the touchstone by which this book tests the Christianity of a work of art. It is art if it earnestly seeks to express, within recognizable artistic canons, that which lies deep within a person's experience; and it is Christian art if that experience itself is Christian.

What Is Church Art?

CHURCH ART IS a specific limitation of Christian art. It is that type of Christian art which is used in churches. It is, for the most part, socialized art; that is, art which affords opportunity to Christians to express their beliefs or emotions together as a group.

Museum art is experienced almost entirely by individuals; home art by families or small groups. Church art must afford expression to large groups of people acting as psychological units. True, church art is not always or necessarily social. Though most Protestants conduct their individual devotions at home rather than in church, Roman Catholics and members of certain other denominations do quite often go to church for their private prayers. Hence the art of those churches has a double burden to carry: individual worship and common worship. Among Protestants, church art is as yet almost entirely for groups worshiping together and not for individuals worshiping alone.

The church building itself is an expression of group feelings. It is the work of many men, generally Christian men. It is used to house a group which is normally expected to be a Christian group. Used as a house of worship, it focuses the eyes and the thoughts of the group upon a central, unifying object or cluster of objects, themselves the product of a long heritage and the result of a mighty group experience of religious faith. The symbolic furniture and designs are looked at by all the people at the same time. The music, whether choral or congregational, is a uniting force. The prayers, even when said by the minister alone, are very definitely the prayers of all. Even the reading of the Bible and the sermon become a group experience when done by a skillful reader and preacher. These are therefore social arts, suitable to give expression to group thought and group emotion.

To the criteria of general and Christian art, church art adds canons of its own. Its primary function is to express the thoughts and feelings of a church group at worship. Everything in a church ought to lead our souls to God. Anything that does not do this should be excluded from church, beautiful or noble as it may be. For in church God is the sole object of men's desiring. Through the arts of the Church people perceive God or have their perception of him heightened; they enter into fellowship with him; and they give expression to certain characteristic Christian responses. Beauty is not the criterion, but worship, and worship alone.

The arts of the Church are numerous. Because life is complex and Christianity is broad and deep, the church arts should be as varied and as catholic (that is to say, as universal) as possible. Why should we deprive ourselves of any form that may help us to give expression to our innermost selves? We do not go to church just to sit and listen, but to place ourselves in a proper relationship to God and to make an intense expression of our souls, in company with our group, to him. We adore, we give thanks, we confess, we implore, we resolve, we dedicate. And these are all actions, actions of the spirit. We give effect to these actions through and by means of certain outward forms. This we could not help even if we would. The inward reality is there before the outward form; but the inner reality comes forth in expressive action by means of form. This is the way men are made. We *must* express our feelings and our moods. Men's moods, like water, seek an outlet. And there is no outlet without the use of form.

Let us remember the purpose of church worship. It is not to seek to move God on our behalf, nor to gain any end for ourselves, nor even to produce anything beautiful. It is simply a means of giving natural expression, in company with our group, to our normal Christian feelings toward God. Our sole effort is to be honest, sincere, and complete in our expression. Worship for worship's sake, as art for art's sake, is therefore a sound theory. Worship or art for beauty's sake is self-destroying. Our quest is to find the most meaningful form by which to express the faith that is within us, not the most ornate, nor the richest, nor the most beautiful, nor the most novel, but the most direct and the most satisfying for the Christian group as a whole or for any part of the group that happens, for the moment, to be worshiping together.

Art thus becomes the medium by which Christians express before God the urges and ideals that cry within them for utterance. Churches which minimize art reduce the means of expression on the part of their worshipers. And when means of expression are reduced or absent, then even the original Christian experiences of the worshipers are in danger of shriveling up and losing their reality.

The Roman Catholics, the Orthodox, and to a lesser extent the Anglicans and Lutherans, recognize this great fact. Though Protestants believe that the Romanists often use symbols and art to convey outworn beliefs, yet the great underlying fact that man naturally uses arts and symbols to express himself is a profound truth that the liturgical churches may teach us all.

Many Protestants have never even thought about this. It is our privilege now to reclaim our heritage. Let the church be the Church; that is, the means by which people come to God in worship. "Then the eyes of the blind shall be opened, and the ears of the deaf shall be unstopped. Then shall the lame man leap as an hart, and the tongue of the dumb shall sing. . . . And an highway shall be there, and a way, and it shall be called the way of holiness." (Isaiah 35:5–8)

CHAPTER II

The Art of Common Worship

IN PRIVATE WORSHIP a Christian may use any form he wishes. He may pray sitting, kneeling, standing, walking, running, riding. He may pray at home, on a mountain top, in bed, on a crowded train, in the kitchen, in the midst of battle. He may read the Bible or other devotional literature, or he may not read at all. He may look at a picture, play the piano, listen to the phonograph, or dance before the Lord. He may use a prayer book or he may make up his own prayers. He may jumble up his confessions and praises, his petitions and dedications. He may use bad grammar or slang. Or he may just sit in receptive silence.

In short, an individual at worship may take any means or method of expressing himself before God that he desires. There are, to be sure, certain laws governing private prayer, based on known constancies of human nature. But any of these laws may be abrogated by any individual at any time, and no one has the right to say that the prayer of such a one is incorrect or unavailing. To maintain this freedom of private methods of prayer is quite essential. To try to change it would be utterly useless.

Common prayer—that is, the prayer of two or more persons—must in some way be ordered so as to hold the thoughts and moods of the worshipers together. "Let us pray"; "Let us sing hymn Number 45"; "Let us unite in the Lord's Prayer"; "Let us attend to the reading of Scripture": these are all directions for the organization, or co-ordination, of common worship. And there are many more, both spoken and unspoken, in every service. Even in Quaker silence there is a drawing together of souls and a more or less uniform progression of thought and feeling. At the end, when the leader arises and shakes hands with his neighbor, he does it not of his own sole volition but because he expresses the sense of the meeting that the climax has been reached and it is time to return to the world.

From Quaker simplicity to the intricacies of the Orthodox or Roman Catholic expressions of group worship may seem to be a long step. And so it is. Yet both extremes, and all intermediate forms, are but means used by groups of Christians to assert their common thoughts, moods, and feelings before God. To learn how and why these varying forms have taken shape is a fascinating study. And to seek to find some service which may ultimately unite all Christians in a truly ecumenical experience of worship, a service which could be engaged in (at least on occasion) and understood in any church in the world, this is one of the most challenging quests upon which any of us could ever embark.

As one looks into the history of the art of worship, one is struck first by the diversity of its means but second, and even more, by the underlying unity of its spirit. The fundamental facts of worship have remained constant, just as have the fundamental canons of all the arts. And the laws of group worship are amazingly similar to the laws of the other arts. First, there is awareness of God's presence as a great objective Being. Without this perception there is no worship. We must have seen him, touched him, listened to him, known him, or experienced him in some manner or other. God is recognized by men in many places: in nature; in the Bible or some great work of art; in the pulsing life of humanity or some individual human, particularly in the priceless career of the historic Jesus; and in the stillness or mighty thunderings of our own inner spirits. Sometimes the view is almost blinding, the tones almost deafening, the touch almost numbing. Awe and wonderment inevitably accompany this mood. But its soul is the simple fact of God's presence. God is! This is the beginning of all worship.

Next comes the sense of relationship. God is Something or Someone whom we can know, with whom we can live, and in whom we do live. What we do we do in his presence; and not only in his presence but in his companionship. This fact is tremendous in its implications.

The third fact is our reaction. Confronted by his greatness and goodness, and thrilled by the privilege of communion with him, we celebrate our joy in adoration and praise; bow in sorrow at our shortcomings; pray that we may live more worthily of him; intercede with him for our friends and for the social well-being and progress of the world; ponder upon all the implications of our faith; and dedicate to him our gifts and our lives. Action is thus the most varied of the three facts of worship. It is the outward expression of our many impulses when we are confronted with God and seek to live in relationship with him. Nevertheless, though action is the most obvious aspect of our common worship, action alone is not worship. Complete worship includes perception and relationship as well as response.

Historically these facts have been recognized by all branches of the Christian faith, and also by many faiths not Christian. In the Christian Church they have been organized into a general order or sequence common to all denominations. There should be a distinct rhythm and balance among these three facts: recognition, fellowship, action. One cannot say that any one of these necessary elements is confined to any one part of the order of worship. All of them are present all the way through. In some parts of the service, especially near the beginning, the recognition aspect is more prominent. In other parts, especially in the latter half, the fellowship aspect. And the active, or expressive phase, pulses rhythmically through the whole.

Earliest Days

THIS ORGANIZATION of our common worship is not an arbitrary scheme invented by any one man or group of men. It goes back into antiquity and seems always to have satisfied naturally the ways of Christian men with their God. In Hebrew days, there had gradually come to be two types of service: that of the synagogue and that of the Temple. The synagogue service was largely a proclamation of the presence of God and instruction to his followers. "Hear, O Israel: The Lord our God is one Lord. And thou shalt love the Lord thy God with all thine heart . . . ," and on through the rest of those glorious passages of recognition, adoration, and good counsel. The reading of the Scriptures, certain authoritative interpretations of them, a sermon, responsive psalms, prayers, and a benediction composed the typical synagogue service. The action was expressed through the responses, chants, and prayers of the people, certain processions of the rabbis and assistants, unveilings of the scroll, standings, gestures, and other motions.

The Temple service was one whose chief emphasis was upon sacrifice. The sacrifice generally took the form of the burning of an edible offering, the animal on the altar standing for the worshiper himself. The worshiper thus vicariously offered up his spirit to be absorbed into the spirit and the life of God. Sacrifice was the entering into a relationship of dedication to God which involved, at its lowest, submission, and at its highest, whole-hearted companionship and understanding. Thus the act of sacrifice had a twofold purpose: offering and fellowship; and yet on their deepest level both of these purposes merge into one. The symbolic action of the worshipers in the service of sacrifice is obvious. The Hebrew scheme bears out the general principle that worship is the threefold fact of the recognition of God, the entering into a particular relationship with him, and the expression of man's reactions to him.

Jesus was a Jew and probably accepted this worship pattern without much criticism. We know that "as his custom was, he went into the synagogue on the sabbath day." And though we cannot speak with the same degree of confidence as to his attitude toward the Temple, we have no evidence that he really opposed it as such. Many scholars think that he initiated the rite of the Lord's Supper, on the night before he died, to take the place of Temple worship. Whether he deliberately did this or not, the fact is that this substitution is what actually happened in Christian history.

The earliest Christians continued to worship in synagogue and Temple. But after opposition arose, and particularly after Gentile Christians began to outnumber Jewish Christians, a gradual withdrawal from the synagogue and Temple naturally ensued. Furthermore, though there were many synagogues, there was but one Temple; and as Christianity became a world religion, contact with the Temple was lost. So it was quite natural that the supper rite of the Christians, so intimately connected both with Jesus' last meal and therefore also with his death and sacrifice, came defi-

nitely to displace the ceremonies of the Temple sacrifice for both
Jewish and Gentile Christians. Nor was it long before the Word
(the synagogue aspect) and the Sacrament (the Temple or
Upper Room aspect—uniting both sacrifice and fellowship) were
included in one service. Ever since, the typical Christian order of
worship has contained both the Proclamation of the Word and
the Celebration of the Sacrament or Holy Supper. Through both
of them ample opportunity for congregational response, expression, and action has been given.

East and West

THE CHRISTIAN WAY of worship was not immedi-
ately standardized into a liturgy. In different places different
emphases naturally arose. Although there are indications in the
New Testament of methods of worship—quotations from prayers,
hymns, creeds, baptism formulae, and the words of institution of
the Lord's Supper—nevertheless the Bible nowhere gives us a
complete order of Christian service.

Until the time of Constantine, the first Christian emperor
(323–337), all the directions for liturgies which have come down
to us are rather simple. Much was left to the judgment of the
individual priest or bishop and there was a large degree of freedom and variety. The *Didache,* a little book of instructions to
churchmen (variously dated from 90 to 130), said: "Allow the
prophets to give thanks as much as they will." But it also gave
suggestions for prayers for those who could not formulate free
prayers. There were numerous Biblical quotations and an order
for the Eucharistic service. Justin Martyr, in his *Apology* (about
150), establishes for us very definitely that by his time the
general pattern of the Service of the Word and the Service of
Sacrament, with characteristic congregational participation and
response, was the norm of church worship.

There have been a number of Eastern liturgies, the chief of
them being that of St. Chrysostom, which is still used in the
Greek and Russian Orthodox churches, and in a few Catholic
churches. In all of these the same general form has been followed.
First there are sentences and prayers of approach, usually of-

fered by the priest in silence. Then there is the Service of the
Word, consisting of adorations, readings, prayers, and instructions; the high point in this service is the "Little Entrance," in
which the Gospels are carried to the altar with ceremony and
reverence. This is followed by the Service of the Sacrament, introduced by the "Great Entrance," at which the holy gifts or offerings are brought forth in solemn procession and placed upon
the altar, and reaching its climax in the prayer of consecration
and the communion. All the way through both the Word service
and the Sacrament service, there are the ceremonial motions and
the verbal and sung responses of the choir and people, and finally
the act of dedication and communion itself.

There are aspects of the Orthodox service which are difficult
for Protestants to understand. The separation of the chancel into
two parts by a screen, called the iconostasis, the priest being
behind the screen saying prayers in silence, and the deacon being
in front of the screen guiding the people in their responses, is a
device which seems quite strange. Once understood, however,
it is quite compatible with our contention that the service of
worship is a recognition of the great fact of God's presence in
the holy of holies, a condition of communion between man and
God, and an act of response on the part of man.

As Christianity spread westward, its services naturally took on
some of the clarity and legalism of the Roman mind. As in the
East so in the West there were from the beginning different
liturgies in different places. In the West the usage of Rome came
gradually to dominate the others; and the power of the papacy
was eventually able almost completely to suppress all other rites
than its own. Although Protestants are in lineal descent from
Rome rather than from Greece, and although in some ways we
can understand and follow the Roman Mass more easily than we
can the Greek Liturgy, nevertheless a comparative study of the
two seems to demonstrate to most Protestant students that the
Greek way is more true to the basic Christian pattern of worship
than that of Rome.

The Roman Catholics gradually came to lose the wholesome
balance between the Word and the Sacrament which they in-
herited from primitive days. The Mass opens, to be sure, on the
same note of adoration and proclamation of God's presence as

do all other services. And, like the others, it also proceeds to a celebration of the Sacrament, which includes both sacrifice and fellowship. The first part, called the service of the catechumens, consists largely of adoration, readings, prayers, and instructions. Though these words are all said or chanted in a low voice and in Latin, the people are taught to follow them in their native languages; and there is generally also a reading of the Gospel and a sermon in the vernacular. The second part, the service of the faithful, is centered in the Sacrament. But the second part so far overshadows the first that the Proclamation of the Word is dull and empty compared to the grandeur and solemnity of the Sacrament. Instead of the two climaxes of the Eastern churches, there is but one in Rome: the miracle of "transubstantiation," or transformation of the bread and wine into the actual body and blood of our Lord. This is accompanied by elevations, the ringing of bells, solemn silences, kneelings, signs of the cross, and other evidences of exalted devotion. Thus the Word is distinctly subordinated to the Sacrament, which becomes the center and soul of the whole Mass.

Furthermore, in the Sacrament itself, the element of fellowship is minimized and that of sacrifice uplifted. Although, as we have seen, fellowship is inevitably present in all true sacrifice, nevertheless the consciousness of healthy fellowship seems to occupy a meager place in the minds of the Roman Catholics. Perhaps this is because it is not so much the sacrifice of the worshiper that is stressed as the sacrifice of Christ. Christ himself is believed to be present on the altar, offering himself again and again in very truth every time the Mass is celebrated. This fact so overwhelms the devout Catholic that the Mass seems to be primarily a matter of adoring this transcendent act of Christ's. Again, the adoration is for the most part limited to this one aspect of Christ's life. His incarnation, character, teachings, activities, and resurrection, though mentioned, all fall into obscurity before the one tremendous fact of his death.

Nevertheless, in spite of the unbalanced structure of the Mass, the three universally recognized facts of Christian worship are most certainly there: perception of God's presence, an entering into relationship between man and God, and a definite response on the part of man to God. Although for the most part we see

more value in the Greek way than the Roman, we must acknowledge the decided superiority of Rome to the East in one
respect: whereas the Eastern service is practically the same day
after day, the Roman has much variety in accordance with the
season of the Christian year. Both of these services have developed along lines of exalted splendor and are highly organized
and sophisticated forms of art. But both are hard to follow unless one is trained in the meanings of the various symbols and
gestures, and of their ancient languages commonly used.

The Protestant Revolt

IF THE MASS emphasizes sacrifice at the expense of
fellowship and the Word, Protestants must be open-minded
enough to note that our services have tended to emphasize the
Word at the expense of both sacrifice and fellowship. This is quite
natural, for the Reformation was a revolt against the failure of
Rome to stress the Word. However, the twist of the wheel carried
the revolution too far. Neither Luther nor Calvin intended it to
turn as furiously as it did. They wanted to restore the balance
which the primitive Church had had and which Rome had lost;
but the balance was soon upset again on the other side. Both
Luther and Calvin, and also the early Anglicans, assumed that
the Lord's Supper would be celebrated every Sunday, along with
the service of the Word. So far did the efforts of these leaders get
out of hand that their followers now generally partake of the
Sacrament only twelve, six, or even four times a year. And in
many churches the sermon so overshadows everything else that
the service has become not much more than a proclamation of the
Word, with little opportunity for Sacrament and still less for responsive action. Indeed the minister is often popularly called the
preacher, the congregation the audience, and the church interior
the auditorium. The minister holds forth; the people listen; the
hard-of-hearing stay at home.

Summarizing our historical sketch, we see that each of the
three main types of Christian worship has faults. The Eastern,
for most of us, is so long and full of ceremony that its accurate
balance and spiritual insight are badly obscured. The Roman,

though briefer and richer in variety, has lost its balance by neglecting the Word and turning the Sacrament into an adoration of Christ's sacrifice. The Protestant services, for the most part, although Protestants have often derided priesthood, have given so exalted a position to the minister that he practically dominates the service with his personality and his words. The Roman and Greek, particularly the Greek, have developed so elaborate a ceremony that it often fails to express modern, straightforward popular thought and feelings; its art has become so riotously complex as no longer to be functional. Protestants, on the other hand, have sought so desperately to purge their services of sham that they have deprived themselves of many legitimate ways of congregational expression.

Our problem today, then, is to search for a norm of common worship which is both traditional and historic in its Christian content, and yet in keeping with modern knowledge; is unafraid of using twentieth-century means of artistic expression; and is simple, clear, brief, and easily understandable by all. The balance between Word and Sacrament must be adequately maintained, and forms cultivated that will tend to give ample opportunity for active expression on the part of the worshiping group.

Again, we must not be satisfied until we come as close as possible to a common path along which we can walk in union and concord with all our fellow Christians everywhere. The general principles of worship are so universally applicable and the desire for unity is at present so widespread, that it ought not to be too difficult to arrange a type of service in which folk of all Christian branches will feel at home. Those Protestants who have sat down in sincerity and openmindedness with their Roman Catholic or Orthodox brothers have been surprised to see how similar are our fundamental ideas about worship. Indeed it is not primarily differences in methods of worship which seem to be keeping us apart but differences in opinion about the validity of the ministry of worship. Yet if we should all learn to worship by means of a type of service which could be understood by all it is inconceivable that such similarity in action would not hasten the day when our ministries as well as our forms of worship would have ecumenical authority. And let us not forget also that in our search for such forms we need not worry as to whether or not they are beautiful. If we seek to become conscious of the presence of God, to enter into a deep and abiding relationship with him and to give him an adequate response, our efforts, all unaware, will take on the clothing of beauty.

THE WORD

Let us consider first the means by which God is to be perceived in church. God's conscious revelation of himself to us with the purpose of having us become aware of him, is assumed as an axiom of our faith. Revelation is an act of God, not man. Man's act is the recognition of it. Thus the minister's first purpose, as the organizer of worship, is to assist men to focus all their perceiving faculties upon God that he may be plainly apprehended by all. If men were always keen and capable, God would need no human priest or minister as interpreter or prophet. But without help men are not always capable, or even desirous, of seeking God. Therefore a service of worship has the responsibility of assisting men to become aware of the revelations which God wishes to make of himself.

The most important way by which most men can see this revelation is through the presentation of the Holy Bible. This, therefore, should be done with much skill, solemnity, and a due sense of its immeasurable importance. It is a very high point in every service. Perhaps the "Little Entrance" of the East could be restored by us. Among some Scottish Presbyterians a deacon or beadle carries the Book in at the beginning of worship. At any rate it should be stationed in a conspicuous place, preferably set off from all other objects; and attention should be called to it at the outset by the minister's going up and opening it before all the people. Colored bookmarks may be used to accentuate its presence; and the reading itself ought to be done in solemn though restrained elocutionary style.

At the announcement of the Gospel reading the people might very well stand, and at the beginning and end give thanks to God. The traditional words at the beginning are, "Glory be to thee, O Lord"; and, at the end, "Praise be to Christ," which may be either spoken or sung. This is very ancient practice and is still quite usable and highly expressive. At various other points in the service, too, more Biblical material than is ordinarily used might well be introduced: in prayers, anthems, hymns, calls to worship, offerings, versicles, ascriptions, and benedictions. Thus should the Word aspect be given fitting expression, the glass cleaned, so to speak, for the people to see God more clearly.

The Sacrament

The sacramental phase of worship, like the Biblical, is not localized in any one place in the service. All of worship is sacramental, even Quaker silence. Technically the Protestant churches have reduced the sacraments to two: baptism and the Lord's Supper. Since baptism is administered but once in a lifetime, the sacramental in worship appears at its clearest in the Lord's Supper. In the Orthodox and Roman Catholic churches today, as it was in the beginning, this is celebrated every Sunday, in many of them every day. To be sure the people in these churches do not receive communion in every service; but the Mass is celebrated, the priest, at least, communicates, and the opportunity is generally open for the people to do so provided they have made the necessary preparations.

The advantages of weekly communion ought seriously to be considered by Protestants; for although it is practiced by the Disciples denomination and by certain other individual churches, it is still very uncommon among most. In the early Church, communion each Sunday was the rule for everyone. Then little by little the priests became lazy and the people careless. By the thirteenth century very few worshipers, even though they regularly attended Mass, thought of taking communion more than once a year. In a sense the priests communicated for the people; but often this did not mean very much to the layman.

Now, however, the Roman Catholic priests are urging more frequent communions upon the people, and the average has risen to perhaps once a quarter or even oftener. Protestants do not have the problem of worshipers not communicating when opportunity is offered; almost all of our worshipers who attend church on communion Sunday actually do take communion. But we do have the problem of infrequent communion services. It is a custom which cannot be overcome quickly. The ministers who read this book could not go back to their churches and decree weekly communion from now on. Much thought and education and perhaps several generations of living are still needed before such a major change can be effected. Nor can it be said that brief early Sunday-morning communion services, such as some churches are now offering, solve the problem; for thus the Word aspect is separated from the sacramental aspect in a way which if long continued might have extremely harmful results.

However, the movement toward more frequent communions, though slow, has already begun. The Lord's Supper on special days, at ordinations, weddings, conferences, and retreats, is far more common than it used to be. And the Christian imagination and sense of fellowship have been stirred very deeply of recent years by the increasing custom of "World-wide Communion" the first Sunday in October. Furthermore, young people particularly are desiring and even demanding more and more frequent cele-brations of this most moving form of religious expression.

Even more important than deciding how often to hold the Lord's Supper is the duty of knowing thoroughly what it is about. The service is a brilliant and many-sided gem. Its aspects are almost inexhaustible. Chiefly it is a communion, a eucharist (or thanksgiving), a memorial, a sacrifice, and a commissioning. Through these many aspects shine forth particularly the two which seem to sum up all the others: communion and sacrifice. These two underlying thoughts should be stressed in all the words, symbols, and actions.

With the Lord's Supper being celebrated in most of our churches only once a month at best, how is the balance between Word and Sacrament to be kept? Until such a day as we shall include them both in every Sunday service, can we not deliber-ately work out some substitute for the Supper to be used when the Supper is omitted? This should not, of course, and cannot be undertaken as a permanent thing; no substitute can ever take the place of the Lord's Supper or be allowed to supersede it. As long as we do have non-communion services, we should seek to arrange them in such a way that something of the value of the complete service will reside in them. To many it would seem as if the offering might well be made the second climax of the service, balancing in solemnity the reading of the Word. At present it is often considered almost as an interlude; people are prone to whisper, look at the printed announcements, or stretch. Some churches, to prevent this, have introduced an anthem or solo here, though often with little thought of giving release to a high mood of whole-souled consecration. But the offering, if well arranged, should come very close to being a real act of sacrament. It combines fellowship and sacrifice and is clothed in a meaningful modern symbol, that of the giving of one's money earnings. To emphasize its importance it ought to be separated from the Word aspect of the service and if local usage will permit, made to come after the sermon. This would help us to leave church with the act of sacrifice and self-dedication vivid in our minds. The hope still is that eventually communion will be celebrated as part of every Sunday-morning service. Lacking such frequent communions, let us find as much sacramental value as possible in the act of public offering.

ACTION

Lack of action is one of the weaknesses of our traditional Protestant services. These gatherings have become in many cases periods of mere sitting and listening, with two or three risings for hymns. Because the worshiper is not asked to do anything, or even, very often, to see anything done, the hour for most people has become rather dull. Let there be more physical action, therefore, for worship itself *is* action. Let the people change their attitudes in the different parts of the service. Let them sit, stand, bow, kneel. In some churches the people walk right up into the chancel for communion; and wherever this is done it seems to have real significance for them. Let them also respond aloud instead of merely listening to the minister pray. And let them be trained to sing audibly and with vigor. Processions and recessions by the choir, and the dignified changing of his place by the minister from his seat to altar or table, to lectern and pulpit, have their influence on the congregation, and show forth motion, joy, determination, and energy.

Let the spiritual actions also be clearly defined and understood. The actions of worship can be reduced to six, not counting private prayer and preparation. The first definite action is adoration: the acknowledgment of the objective fact of God's presence in infinite glory, majesty, and goodness. With this can be included praise and thanksgiving. A processional hymn of adoration, Biblical sentences, the *Doxology*, a Psalm, the *Gloria*, and possibly also a brief anthem of praise are obviously expressive of this mood of awareness. Secondly comes confession, to be followed by an assurance of forgiveness and the Lord's Prayer. Confession should be made in unison to indicate the social nature of the sins which we acknowledge in church. Then follows the setting forth of God's Word by the reading of the Gospel, by a hymn of faith or exhortation, and by the sermon. The sermon should keep just as closely as possible to the business of explaining the Scripture and of exhorting people to live in its spirit, and should not be lengthy or involved. The fourth action is prayer, including a devotional hymn, petitions, and intercessions, and possibly an anthem of a quiet and supplicatory nature. The offering should if possible come next, employing a period of silence, fellowship and dedication, and concluding with a recessional hymn of consecration and adventure in God's service. Finally the benediction and a season of quiet prayer send the congregation forth in peace and serenity, confidence and joy.

The above is the normal service without the Lord's Supper. When the communion is celebrated, the order is the same up to and including the sermon. After this comes the hymn of devotion, the invitation, the petitions and intercessions, the offering of alms, the *Sursum Corda* and *Sanctus* ("Lift up your hearts" and "Holy, holy, holy!"), the eucharistic prayer, the narrative of institution, communion, thanksgiving, recessional hymn of dedication, and benediction.

Thus, whether the service of money-offering or the service of communion is celebrated, the sequence of acts, on the part of the congregation, is the same: namely, adoration (including praise and thanksgiving); confession; thoughtfulness in the presence of God's Word; prayer; fellowship and sacrifice; and quietness under God's blessing. These six acts of worship should be understood by the people. Everyone should know where one phase begins and the other leaves off. It should be thoroughly realized by all that these actions are but a natural response on the part of the congregation to the other two great facts of worship, namely, awareness of God's presence and relationship with him.

A fair-minded appraisal will show that such a service is not overelaborate. It attempts to be complete, summarizing all our natural moods, thoughts, and emotions before God; but each part should be brief, understandable, and straight to the point. The fault with the traditional Protestant service is that some parts of it, notably the sermons, pastoral prayers, and anthems, have been flagrantly embellished and lengthened, while other essential parts of worship have been ignored. The balance and rhythm have been upset and true simplicity lost. The history of the Church as a whole should recall us to the necessity of completeness; but our study of effective artistic expression should hold us to dignity, purity, and sincerity. We cannot disregard the fact that common worship is, both for the leader and for the congregation, a high art, and should follow well-established artistic canons, including the canon of simplicity. By means of these forms of expression we both show forth our inner selves to God and also, by opening ourselves to him, deepen our spiritual lives. There is nothing in all life that is more important for us to learn than the art of common worship.

CHAPTER III

The Church Building

THE MOST OBVIOUS object of church art is the building where Christians gather for their acts of social worship. This building must be of approximately the right size for the congregation which habitually uses it. It must be strong enough to withstand the attacks of nature and, sad to say, of man also, if possible. It must be adequately lighted, properly tempered as to warmth and coolness, and equipped with the necessities and conveniences that its occupants demand of it. All this is clear.

But what then? Can a person not worship God in a bare barn as successfully as in what George Fox called a "steeple house"? Thirty million dollars for a cathedral indeed! Are not hospitals, schools, or even battleships more useful? We must build churches, to be sure, but will the additional luxuries of beauty and adornment bring us any closer to God? Is not the simplest expression always the best?

Line upon Line

WELL, LET US SEE. We must remember throughout our discussion that the function of a church building is to aid people to see God, to feel a relationship with him, and to engage in the expressive actions of worship. If the building accomplishes this purpose, it is successful; if not, it is a failure.

Let us begin our inquiry by considering the meaning of a line. We cannot put up a wall, or insert in the wall a window, or impose upon it a roof, or support it with a buttress, or hang upon it a curtain, or place before it a piece of furniture, without dealing with lines. Lines may be vertical, horizontal, curved, or broken. Human nature being what it is, these lines give expression to varying thoughts or moods in our spirits. A vertical line expresses aspiration; a horizontal line serenity; a curved line graciousness; a broken line conflict. Though one type generally predominates in any given edifice, almost all buildings combine all four. A Georgian church, for instance, having a low roof with a triangular pediment, may also have cylindrical pillars, a rounded interior arch at its head end, and a curved ceiling. These lines are structural; one cannot avoid use of structural lines.

An architect must study to see that his building fulfills if possible its essential purpose. One who is careless, or not a Christian, may not know enough about the Christian spirit to know how to arrange his lines so that this spirit is given expression. The eye naturally follows a line. In many of our churches lines are at cross-purposes. They are broken, lead nowhere, interrupt other lines, confuse vision, scatter thoughts, and bewilder emotions. Other churches, on the other hand, seem to be built in just such a way as to give ready expression to the feelings of joy, peace, thoughtfulness, aspiration, and consecration.

Besides the problems of line in church architecture, there are problems of material, color, texture, space, balance, weight, and tension, all of which are basic. An architect has to be engineer, mason, carpenter, painter, mathematician, electrician, plumber; he needs to be expert in heating, lighting, and a dozen other subjects; and in addition to these should be an historian, financier, psychologist, philosopher, and Christian. All of these skills have to be employed in such a manner as to give to the group for which he builds as complete an opportunity as possible to give expression to the characteristic releases of Christian worship. The job of architect, like the function of the church he creates, is complex and many-sided.

Pre-Christian Days

The study of architectural origins takes us back into the shadowy time before the writing down of history. Dwellings, tombs, and temples quite naturally came into being before all other structures. Necessity pressed for shelter; religion for tombs and temples. The three widely separated centers of China, India, and the valleys of the Tigris, Euphrates, and Nile seem to have been the areas where formal architectural style was first developed.

The three Near Eastern civilizations were obviously related. All of them sought to express in their structures the ideals of power, solidity, and durability. The earliest temple was no doubt a circle of stones, bricks, or earth. Solid walls followed. Columns then gave the enclosures dignity. Roofs were added and porticoes formed. Simple rectangular towers and high outdoor altars for astronomical observations and sacrifices were among the first erections within the enclosures. Later these temples blossomed forth into spacious courts with mighty buildings, colonnades, obelisks, vistas, gateways, pools, towers, inner shrines, priestly homes, symbols, relief work, statues, and paintings. Eventually such grandeur became almost overwhelming.

In Greece dignity and harmony distinguished the temples of the pre-classical period. With the development of the Doric into the Ionic, Corinthian, and Hellenistic styles, ornamentation increased until finally Greek buildings also came to be clothed in a mass of decoration. Indian and Chinese architecture followed somewhat the same development. Yet the Greeks and the Chinese, more than the Indians or Egyptians, were able to maintain throughout the centuries the essential simplicity of line which is characteristic of their earliest structures. The ornament is superficial. All the structural lines of the buildings are visible, strong, and honest.

Among the Hebrews too, though we know all too little about their buildings, ornamentation seems to have grown more prominent as civilization became more complex. The descriptions of the Temple in I Kings and II Chronicles say more about its carvings and furnishings, its gold and precious wood, its jewels and fabrics, than they do about its essential lines. The lines themselves, nevertheless, seem to have been plain and straightforward; and except for the carved cherubim, oxen, and floral designs, there were no pictures or statues.

The Romans believed in order and balance just as fully as the Greeks. The earliest Roman temples were mere copies of Greek styles. Domes came later possibly through Roman observations

in the Near Eastern countries which they had conquered; and
Roman engineering skill raised these domes to unprecedented
size and height. Rounded arches also developed, possibly from
Asia Minor through the Etrusians. The Romans had no strong
or attractive religion of their own, setting them off from other
people, and thus their religious architecture, although distinctive,
was largely eclectic.

The Christian Touch

THE FIRST CHRISTIAN groups worshiped happily
in any kind of structure which happened to be available, whether
synagogues, private homes, or public basilicas. Before long, special
buildings were erected. The form of the cross as a ground plan,
though never universal, quite naturally came to be popular both
in Rome and in the Near East. In the East, domes, instead of
being confined to circular apartments as in Rome, came to be
placed over the intersections of these cross-shaped buildings and
often also at the ends of the transepts, covering square spaces or
rooms. The number of domes used in the same building grew
greater as time went on. Supports and columns were diversified.
Mosaics on gold background began to be incrusted upon vaults
and walls. The result of these changes was what we know as the
Byzantine style. In the West, towers—first one, then more—were
added, sometimes attached to the building, sometimes adjoining
it. Vaulting became complex. Mural paintings were more common than mosaics.

As Christianity spread into northern Europe, it took with it both
Byzantine and Roman forms. Russia built domes, and France
arches and vaulting, with new daring. Each brought into being
a style of building so different from its predecessor that many
have called the results entirely new creations. But Russian style
is a development of Byzantine, as modified by the northern,
wooden, shedlike native buildings, while Gothic is a development of the Romanesque.

The French, obsessed by the desire for height and interior
color, reached ever upward, with stories and clerestories, to

provide more and more windows. As whole cities sometimes wished to attend church in a body in the Middle Ages, wide spaces as well as great light areas were required. Out of these needs grew the Gothic style, with ribbed vaulting, slender supports, arched windows, and flying buttresses. The structure of the church became but a skeleton. Higher and higher was the vault raised; more and more slender became the columns; and more and more gorgeous the windows which took up most of the spaces between the actual supports in the walls. Depth, perspective, color, and lighting effects became utterly majestic. Though the Gothic style was ornamented in much greater profusion than either the Greek or Romanesque had been, its tremendous height and vast reachings absorbed the rich detail. Essentially the Gothic, like its predecessors, had unity, consistency, and integrity; it retained the visibility of its main structural lines.

Little save variation on the Greek, Roman, and Gothic styles has been attempted in church architecture until very recently. The Georgian churches, developed in England under the Georges, have been popular in America, especially in New England, since Colonial times. They are basically Roman, but the addition of steeples gave this style a special grace and charm. A revival of Greek influence further modified the forms of these churches after about 1820.

In our own generation a new type of building, called for want of a better name, "functional," "international," or "modernistic," has come into being. New materials, such as steel, alloys, and glass bricks, and such developments as central heating, electric lighting, and ventilation have afforded startling new possibilities to our architectural creativity. The churches, especially in America, have been slower than commercial firms to avail themselves of these opportunities; yet some have done so, and it is safe to say that more will. One of the chief triumphs of the modernist is his ability to create great spaces in our buildings without the use of columns or vaults. Simplicity of structure, combined with thin walls, wide doors and windows, and great depth and height, with fireproofing throughout, can now be attained as never before. It would seem that we who live in these days of vast motion-picture theaters, streamlined railroad stations, and uncluttered concert halls, would want to transfer some of the best features of these buildings to our churches. Perhaps it is just because these other types of social artistry utilized modernism before the Church did that we have been reluctant to employ the same devices in church. Since most of our new Protestant churches are small, we do not need the modern style so much as our Romanist friends do. But even small churches in this new style have greater interior visibility and better acoustics, boldness of color, and economy of line.

It is noteworthy that, though Christianity has vivified and changed much that it has touched, it has usually left the fundamental lines of old styles unaltered. Christianity is so varied, even within a denomination of such rigid regulations as the Roman, that Christians of equal sincerity, depth of feeling, and intelligence, can express their thoughts and emotions through many different forms. Mosques, synagogues, and pagan temples have been turned into churches more than once; and the process has also been reversed. In mission fields, native, non-Christian styles are often utilized by Christians. In Europe and America, Greek, Romanesque, Gothic, and modernistic forms, and their many variations, have all been successfully used. The fact seems to be that any building of unified, strong, honest structure can be employed as a place of divine worship. We seem, then, to be drawn to the conclusion that it is the symbols, the choice and placement of furniture, the ornamentation and coloring, more than the style or structural lines themselves—provided only that these lines be not weak, confused, or disturbing—which give distinctive expression to the Christian spirit in a church building.

Windows and Light

WINDOWS SHOULD CONFORM to the architectural style of a building. In a classic church, clear plain windows are the most suitable. In an environment which would let in incongruous views, such windows should be translucent or lightly curtained. If there are curtains, whether used to cover or to flank windows, they should be of a cool or neutral shade, and in harmony with the walls. If tinting is used in clear glass, it should be slight; and the woodwork or leadwork should follow the simple, rectangular lines of the building itself.

In a Gothic structure, where windows often occupy most of the wall space, some tempering of the garish light is necessary; hence the use of colored glass. Stained glass, if good, cannot but be expensive. The effects attained by painted, or "art," glass— a late and generally unworthy development of the Gothic period —are almost always unfortunate. Realistic pictures should be avoided; they distract attention from the common acts of worship during service; and rarely induce a prayerful spirit. Moreover, glass is not a natural or proper medium for painted pictures. A profusion of rich colors—particularly deep reds, blues, purples, and greens—in formal, stylized, or two-dimensional pictorial designs, is much preferable.

The common notion that the windows in medieval churches were primarily intended to be the picture books of the people, instructing them in the history of the Bible and the saints, is open to serious question. Most of the great medieval windows are stylized. Their purpose was artistic, not didactic. In a modern church, there is certainly no adequate reason to use the windows as bulletin boards for painted angels, saints, or even Biblical heroes. If we wish to exhibit paintings in a church—which should be done only with great caution—let them be upon canvas, wood, or plaster; or let us hang some of the splendid colored prints now available. In a modern Gothic church as in a medieval one, windows should be for the chief purpose of letting in a variegated, richly colored, gay, religious light, expressing the mystical and joyous aspects of the moods of worship. Their designs should not be in so obvious or mathematical a style as to call attention to themselves. A small, well-conceived, and skillfully executed medallion, either round or oblong, hung in the middle of a window of clear glass, is enormously preferable to a larger window of unworthy artistry. Properly employed there is nothing more conducive of worship in certain types of church than the luxuriant beauties of colored glass. If a visitor wishes to examine the windows in detail for their symbolic subtleties, saintly representations, or instructional values, let him do so either before or after the service of worship.

Artificial interior lighting is a subject which requires careful study in each local situation. The average Protestant service takes place in the brightness of high morning; but preparation must also be made for cloudy days and evening services. If possible, the congregation should be allowed to have enough daylight to read in comfort. Where such natural light needs to be augmented, either indirect lighting or visible fixtures which harmonize inconspicuously with the interior may be used. Good fixtures are expensive, and even at best most types are hard to keep clean and filled with bulbs. Indirect lighting is therefore often both better and more practical.

Though the nave of the church should be comfortably illuminated, the greatest concentration of light ought to be in the chancel. All the chief symbols of worship, and at the appropriate time, their ministers, should be clearly—even strikingly—in view. The chancel should have more light than merely that needed for reading. It is essential, however, that no lights stronger than candle lights shine into the eyes of the people; these distract attention and irritate the nerves. Lights ought to be controlled by rheostat if possible, the operator being an usher who is especially fitted, not only technically but artistically and spiritually, to manage such an important aid to worship. Sometimes his impulse, and this alone, will prompt him as to how much light is needed at a given point in a service. But his impulse should be the result of long experience and a worshipful nature.

Where the financial resources of the church permit, experimentation may also be made in the effects of different colors both on walls, in ornaments, and in lights. Very little is known about this subject as yet; but psychologists would no doubt be as willing to help churches, if they were asked, as they are to serve commercial shops and factories. This matter will be referred to again in a later chapter.

Landscaping

THE EXTERIOR OF a church, even though good in itself, is frequently marred by an inadequate setting. City situations often afford no opportunity for landscaping whatsoever. In such cases adjoining public or commercial buildings have some-

times been commendably planned to harmonize with the style of
the church. Some local governments forbid the erection of other
buildings which obstruct the view, or have even torn down such
obstacles and created parks, squares, or greens about their handsome churches. Other communities, on the other hand, seem to
place convenience of traffic or mercantile profit before everything else.

If there is some land about a church, the situation should be
carefully analyzed and the advice of a landscape gardener se-
cured to meet its needs and fulfill its possibilities. There are
churches whose ugliness needs to be clothed; others whose beauty
is too much hidden. Well-meaning people have often planted
memorial trees or shrubs in haphazard fashion, not remembering
that they will surely grow. After sentiment has attached itself
to such plantings, it is difficult for a committee or a pastor to
effect their removal. Individual plants often do not harmonize
with other plants; vines grow on the wrong surfaces or are too
lush or of unsuitable texture; or shadows hang heavily over windows or upon stone or dark colored walls. The walks and doorways should always be inviting and of easy access, and façades
and spires open to unobstructed view. Exterior signboards ought
to be in harmony with the church architecture; beware of standardized models. The character and design of both building and
background should form a unified whole, speaking invitingly of
peace, contemplation, stability, power, and aspiration. Even way-
farers who do not stop for worship may have their thoughts lifted
to the things of God by the concord of the scene; and those who
habitually attend the services will find a physical welcome which
places them in a suitable mood for the spiritual experiences which
they anticipate upon their entrance into church.

Church gardens are becoming more and more thought of as
aids to spiritual recreation. A secluded plot behind a wall or
hedge, with a formal or a rustic cross, an outdoor pulpit and
sloping terrace for meetings, a pool or birdbath, a statue of St.
Francis and the birds, cloisters and benches for rest and thought,
would be of priceless value to many people, especially in town
or city. If a church wishes to sponsor a tennis court or children's
playground, these should be kept quite separate from the garden
of contemplation.

The conclusion of the whole matter of architecture is this: a church building forms the physical home of a worshiping community. Hence its whole bodily structure, and the construction and placement of every single part and object in or about it, should have but one sole purpose; namely, to enable the group to express its thoughts and feelings in the fullest possible way in the worship of eternal God. Where the architecture and landscaping assist in this function they are successful; where they do not, no matter how intrinsically beautiful or useful they may be, they fail to fulfill their reason for existence.

CHAPTER IV

Fittings and Furnishings

THE CHARACTER OF a building is often established by its ornament and furniture even more than by its structural qualities. Ornamentation may make all the difference as to whether a given edifice can really be called Christian or not. The Hebrew scrolls, the Buddhist or Hindu images, the Confucian tablets, the Mohammedan prayer niches, the Orthodox iconostases, the Roman Catholic stations of the cross, the Baptist fonts, are all unmistakably distinctive, no matter what the type of building in which they reside. There are even concert halls and theaters whose interiors would not distinguish them from churches apart from the furniture and symbolic decorations used. This does not mean, however, that we may disregard strength and integrity of line, or, on the other hand, that we must keep on piling up symbols, pictures, and carvings.

A rule as good as it is ancient is that there should be no embellishments except those which are necessary for use, convenience, or propriety. Though some types of building can stand much more such elaboration than others, all should be adorned and furnished with restraint. A church is not a museum for the display of heterogeneous and unrelated objects of Christian art. We must know precisely what it is we want to do when we go to church, and why; and even the smallest detail must further that purpose or be banished.

Roman Catholics, though their churches are apt to err more than Protestant houses of worship in their tendency to overelaboration, can nevertheless give a clear answer to many questions upon which Protestants are still divided and groping. In the Catholic church all interest is focused upon the altar, where the holy drama takes place. Here are the relics of the saint. Here the miracle is performed in every Mass. Here Christ himself is present for the worshipers to behold and adore, repeating his sacrifice at every service of worship. Here the Epistle and Gospel are read, the priest facing the altar as he reads. Although other functions of worship—baptism, preaching, personal prayer before the stations of the cross, various types of private and public devotion—are also performed in church, they are all so overshadowed by the miracle at the altar that there is no question in anyone's mind as to where the eyes of every worshiper should be led.

There are movements now abroad among Roman Catholics to simplify the appurtenances of the sanctuary, to get rid of the tawdry colors, paper flowers, garish statues and multiplicity of candles and other eye-catching details which mar and clutter so many of their churches, and to relegate the stations of the cross to a special room. There is even a suggestion to remove the reredos, bring the altar closer to the laity, place the priest behind it, facing the people, as in early Christian days, and restore the choir to the chancel. But never, even in a wild or unguarded moment, has any Catholic suggested that the altar itself with its essential furnishings be left out of a church or shifted to any other position than that which holds the center of attention. In Greek and Russian churches there is only one altar. In Roman churches there may be many; but one in particular is always lifted up, and central. Without the altar there can, indeed, be no Mass. The Roman liturgical philosophy is secure, completely accepted by all, and integrated around this one dominating idea. Hence a Roman Catholic feels at home in any church in the world which he may enter.

Members of the free churches, on the other hand, are at present going through a period of unsettlement. Though the movements among us have not reached revolutionary proportions nor become unified around any one doctrine, there is in many churches much dissatisfaction with things as they are. The Victorian pattern is slowly passing. This arrangement included a central pulpit, with its Bible, and three chairs, on a platform; then the choir, raised and facing the people; and lastly the organ pipes. The console was often behind the pulpit, the organist thus having his back to the minister. Though the majority of free churches still retain this arrangement, many new ones are now being built with an altar or table in the center of the head end, a divided choir flanking the altar, and a middle aisle leading toward it. Many old churches are also being rearranged in this way.

Although this general pattern seems to be emerging, there are still many differences in detail. Sometimes there is an altar with a cross upon it, close to the end wall or attached to a reredos so that the minister and deacons cannot sit behind it. Sometimes the altar stands out from the wall, with minister's and deacons' chairs to its rear. During communion service the minister in such churches stands behind the altar and is partially hidden by the cross; but in some cases the cross is removed on communion Sundays so that the minister can be seen. Frequently there is a table, with a cross upon it. Sometimes there is an altar or table without the cross, in which case a cross is often suspended above, or fixed on the wall behind. Occasionally a globe is to be seen in the center of the table, or a fern, or a bouquet of flowers, or an open Bible, picture, or seven-branched candlestick. In a few cases there is both an altar and a table, the altar being at the far end and the table at the near end of the chancel. In one case a table has been observed as a detachable part of an altar, to be drawn forth on communion Sundays. Some denominations must also think of the necessity of making room for a large baptismal font, which they often try to hide or disguise when not in use. Free churches have no rubrics and therefore one does not know what he will find on entering a Protestant meetinghouse.

Faith and Furniture

AMID SUCH CONFUSION as has been pointed out, the chief common factor is vigorous thought, which is bound to bring disagreements in detail. However, our movements seem to be taking us all more or less in the same general direction: namely, toward a renewed emphasis upon the sacramental aspect of our worship. The issue is basically a theological one and must be treated as such.

Three preliminary points may assist us in our thinking. First: no church ought to make any change at all until it knows pretty well what it is doing and why. It is usually better to leave things

as they are than to introduce innovations which may have to be
changed again with the next minister or the next prudential committee or session. The only way to decide what should be done to
make a church functionally worshipful is to know what we mean
by our religion and by our worship, and then to seek to give expression to that. In the meanwhile churches ought surely to be
studying the fundamental problems concerned. Second: the issue
must not be decided by the architect alone, nor on grounds of
beauty alone. Art merely for beauty's sake is not a sufficiently
worthy attitude. Design and adornment have a definitely worshipful function to perform. It is not Christian to seek to impress
people with wealth, grandeur, decorum, or taste: a church building is not to be admired but to lead people to express their souls
toward God. Third: because our aim is worshipful expression, we
should therefore study to develop and maintain the skills and
canons of true art; for in thus doing we shall give ever more adequate representation to our worshipful motives and urges. If we
follow these simple rules, we shall doubtless also find that beauty
has been added unto us as an unpremeditated extra gift. Let us,
then, pause to review the three fundamental facts of worship
which we have already considered, and seek to discover some
applications from them.

OUR PERCEPTION OF GOD

First: worship is the perception of God, eternal, majestic, infinite in power, goodness, and truth. Our church interiors should
seek to make people cognizant of the limitless reality of this Being. Two predominant opportunities are at our disposal here: the
careful placing of the major symbols and the development of a
feeling of depth.

There are four chief artistic symbols of God's revelation of himself to man. Most Protestants would put the Bible first. This
therefore should be prominently mounted in plain sight. Considering its extraordinary importance, one's first impulse is to
place the Bible on a central stand in the axial line of the church.
But the Bible is not the only symbol, and one may hardly favor a
disposition which will subordinate all other symbols to this one.
The table, to which Christ invites all his disciples, is an equally
potent symbol of God's self-revelation. If the table, also on the

axial line, is placed in front of the Bible and pulpit, at the head of a wide center aisle and in a broad space cleared of pews so that everyone is enabled to see it, perhaps it may succeed in maintaining a fair degree of parity with a central Bible, even though the table is on a lower level. There is much to be said for the intimacy of having the table down near the people, provided they can see it plainly and recognize it for what it is. Generally the table, when placed before the pulpit—especially if there is no center aisle—is not conspicuous or even visible to the worshipers beyond the first few pews. A better place for the table than this might therefore be sought.

The third symbol is the pulpit, station of God's prophet or preacher. The pulpit, if possible, should be differentiated from the lectern which holds the Bible. The fourth symbol is the cross, by which God in Christ showed forth his suffering and redemptive love. The best disposition of these four symbols would seem to be that which keeps a balance of them all. To do this the cross may be placed upon the far wall; the table on the axial line of the chancel, several steps above the main floor level and well out from the wall; the lectern, with its Bible, to one side; and the pulpit of the living prophet to the other side. Thus the sacrifice and fellowship of the Sacrament, and the historicity and prophetical vigor of the Word are kept in equipoise, all showing forth the infinite greatness of our God.

Benches or stalls for minister and deacons or elders, may be ranged behind the table, the central one being slightly higher backed than the others but not visible above the table. It would be well to tie the whole together with paneling on the far wall or a dossal curtain, of the width at least of the table's length, beginning at a suitable height and descending all the way to the floor. The cross, whether based upon a ledge of the paneling or hanging before the curtain, should be entirely above the head of a standing minister.

The other physical factor which can aid the people to be acutely aware of the presence of God is a long unbroken prospect. When a company gathers to worship outdoors, it invariably seeks a hillside, or a lake shore, or a clearing in the woods. In any room it is natural to arrange the chairs so that they face not walls but spaces. It is an ineradicable tendency for people to seek the back seats in church. Ministers should not scold people for this but rather try to understand their psychological requirements for a clear view and rich perspective. For this reason the pews should always face the length of the room and not be curved. Anything that blocks the physical outlook tends to block also the mind and the spirit. The table should be low enough not to interfere with the prospect. A pulpit should not be too high and conspicuous. The eyes of the worshipers should not be focused on any single one of the symbols —cross, Bible, table, pulpit—but on the group of these as a whole in a setting of depth. It would be well to have no railing or screen obstructing the people's access or view to the chancel. If a screen is desired for historic reasons, let it be a high rood screen, or beam.

A chancel, while not mandatory, offers an extended vision suggestive of the measurelessness of God's beauty. The word comes from the same Latin root as "cancel." It originally meant a lattice which separated one portion of a room from another. The typical historical church consisted of three parts: the narthex, or vestibule, for non-communicants and penitents; the nave, for members; the chancel, for priests and choir. The chancel, in turn, is divided into two parts: the choir, and at the extreme end, the sanctuary. Symbolically the narthex and nave represent the world; the chancel, heaven. The effect of arranging the head end of the room as a chancel—concentrating therein most of the articles of worship in their proper balance, and causing the choir and clergy stalls to face in toward the axis at right angles to the congregational pews—is that the depth of the room seems extended even though nothing is done to change the architectural lines themselves. In some churches there is a cross on the lattice, or rood screen, illustrating the fact that a Christian in his pilgrimage and warfare must inevitably pass under the cross in order to enter everlasting life. Such symbolism may seem somewhat forced to Protestants; but the basic idea of a chancel is suggestive of holiness, eternity, infinity. Gazing down its reaches we are led to a contemplation of the things that pass not away.

OUR RELATIONSHIP WITH GOD

Secondly, worship is not only a perception of God but a relationship to him. The group, held together by its spiritual fellowship, communes, both as a group and as individuals, with God.

The central table, out from the wall, with stalls and pews clustering about it, is the chief symbol of this fact of fellowship. A table implies community; it unites. Pastor, deacons, choir, and people, caught up in the Spirit, hold high fellowship with one another and with God and his Christ, around that precious table. Let none make the table into an altar without thinking of the peril of weakening or even losing this sense of holy communion.

Our Response to God

Finally, worship is action. Some of this action can be undertaken with eyes closed. Architecture and symbolism are not always essential. But most of our spiritual action can be heightened by a visual setting which is designed to be a natural conductor for it. Thanksgiving for God's goodness in the realm of nature, for instance, can the more readily be effected when we see before us well arranged groupings of greens or flowers. The offering of sacrifice, though always difficult, ought to be easier before either an altar or a cross. Furthermore, spiritual expression may often be aided by actual physical motion.

In planning a church, plenty of room should be left for all the characteristic actions of worship. For many of these a platform is scarcely adequate. Since a central pulpit and a fixed, central throne for the pastor make dramatic action almost impossible, the minister should be supplied with a stall at one side, inconspicuous and next to the choir. As much of the worshipful action of the congregation as possible ought to be done without his leadership. When singing a hymn of adoration, a congregation should not be compelled to look at him but at the symbols of God himself. But when, in the course of a service, the minister does come out from his stall, he should have space to proceed with dignity to table, pulpit, lectern, prayer bench, or wherever the action calls for his presence at the moment. For the reception of new members, there ought to be room enough for all to gather uncrowded around the table. In communion, if worshipers can go right up into the sanctuary, so much the better. Long benches may be placed on communion Sundays just in front of the choir stalls. Sitting so close to the table, most persons would receive communion with greater devotion and joy. There ought also to be plenty of space for all the members of the party in a service of matrimony, or in an ordination or commissioning service. The chancel ought therefore to be spacious, both in width and depth. It could well take up a far larger proportion of the floor space than at present it does, for the days when every available inch had to be used for congregational seats are gone. In small churches even a third of the room might be given over to the chancel.

The Language of Symbols

WHY IS IT that one often visits churches where the national and church flags are eagerly displayed but where it is nevertheless considered too "Catholic" to erect a cross? This surely exhibits a confusion of thought. If a church does not approve of symbols at all—which is a difficult position to hold—then let it have neither flag nor cross. But if a church does approve of symbols, then the primary Christian symbol ought not to be omitted and others allowed.

The truth of the matter seems to be that no church is devoid of symbolism. The building itself is a symbol; the word "nave" means a ship, the ark by which we all travel the seas of life. The steeple is a symbol, as is the cross on the steeple, if there is one. The Bible, the pulpit, the table or altar, the arrangement of chairs and furniture, vestments or their absence, flowers, lights, colors— all have symbolic import.

In this country it has come to be considered that a simple Latin cross on a church denotes Roman Catholicism, a cross with a circle Episcopalianism, and a weather vane a free church. But there is no reason why any sect should be given a monopoly of the cross or any type of the cross. The cross is something which should be a uniting rather than a dividing sign; and its display on church exteriors should therefore be encouraged. The weather vane never was a Christian symbol. It was erected for the purpose of forecasting the weather in isolated, agricultural communities, and is now out of date and superfluous. A rooster on a roof is justified both historically and intrinsically; for it signifies the preacher rising up early in the morning to carry the Word to the world.

Durandus reminds us that the preacher, like the cock, must always beat himself before he crows! Still the cross is the most suitable sign to surmount a Christian church. Symbols are outward signs of inner convictions or feelings. They are language, as truly as words are language, and often they are far more potent than words.

In a church, symbols have a twofold direction—they are agents for God to show himself to us, and they are agents by which we express ourselves to God. In either case a symbol cannot be a method of communication unless it has meaning to the people who use it. Hence symbols should always be explained to children and newcomers until they are thoroughly understood. Unless this is done there is great peril in symbols. We must guard against the danger of ignorance as against a deadly plague. If the signs and art language of the church are learned by the people then they are an open door to new richness of expression.

The symbols which Christians have used in the course of the ages are multitudinous. At times they seem to be almost too varied and intricate. Even the vocabulary of symbolism is complex. Distinction is made between symbols, emblems, figures, and attributes. In general a *symbol* is something which stands for or represents something else; but a Christian symbol is also defined in the more restricted sense as a representation which is sanctioned by Biblical or ecclesiastical authority. A symbol may be an object, picture, design, story, person, or act.

An *emblem* is that which, by reason of natural fitness rather than of outer authority, typifies some object or quality other than itself. Thus a circle, for reasons quite obvious, is an emblem of eternity or of endless love. A *figure* is an arbitrary invention showing forth some analogy or metaphor. Grapes, or a pelican, or a fish, have often been used as figures of our Lord. An *attribute* is the mark of a quality residing in some person or which signifies his character, office, or personal identity. A lion is employed as an attribute of saints who met death in the amphitheater or who showed remarkable courage in some exploit; a dove is an attribute of men of peace or of those who have been inspired of God. These words are often used loosely or interchangeably; and the general term *symbol* may include them all.

Certain objects may be symbols, emblems, figures, and attributes, or any two or three of them, at the same time. Thus the dove, in addition to being an attribute of certain types of people, is also, by divine action [1] the symbol of the Holy Spirit, as well as being an emblem of the human spirit. In this last capacity it has often been pictured as representing a soul emerging from the mouth of a dying Christian. The lion is a symbol of our Lord—the Lion of the tribe of Judah—but it is also an attribute of St. Jerome and other desert saints, and an emblem of strength and power. The cross is a symbol of Christ, an emblem of our redemption, a figure of the Church, and an attribute of a sacrificial life.

Of the other symbols of Jesus, the most common are the lamb, the vine, the bread, the door, the sun, the star, the light, the rock. The fish, earliest of them all, usually a dolphin because of the love which the Greeks had for it, had many felicitous associations. For one thing its letters formed an anagram for the Greek phrase, "Jesus Christ, Son of God, Savior." Furthermore, it reminded Christians of the water of baptism and of Jesus' invitation to his disciples to become fishers of men. The lamb, when a symbol of Jesus, has a tri-radiated nimbus and carries a banner of the cross triumphant. The pelican was used, especially in the later Middle Ages, as a figure of Jesus because of the belief that it was willing to pluck its own breast to feed its young with life-giving blood. The crown is also an emblem of Jesus, as well as of Mary and of many saints and martyrs.

Of all the symbols of our Lord the cross is now the most common. It was first employed in the fourth century, and by the tenth it had superseded the fish. It was about the sixth century that the image of Christ was first placed upon it, and not until the thirteenth that this came into common use. The crucifix is now required to be placed over the altars of all Roman Catholic and of many other churches, though from Passion Sunday to Good Friday crucifixes are generally veiled. There are many different kinds of crosses: the simple Latin cross; the Greek cross, in which the four arms are of the same length; the St. Andrew's cross, in the form of the letter X; the Tau cross, shaped like a T; the Maltese cross, with spreading arms of equal length; the Celtic cross, having short arms connected by a circle; the swastika, which

[1] Mark 1:10.

was also used in pre-Christian and is still used in certain non-Christian religions; and many variations and elaborations of these forms.

Standing crosses are frequently mounted upon graded bases, generally with three steps. These steps are said to refer to the three virtues of faith, hope, and charity, and also signify the climb up the hill of Calvary. Altar crosses often bear the I H S (or I H C) or *Chi Rho* monograms, or the lamb, in the center. On the top bar a tablet is sometimes affixed with the letters I N R I, signifying the kingship of Jesus. These literary symbols will be further explained in a later chapter. A cross with a double bar is the emblem of an archbishop or patriarch, and sometimes of a cardinal. It is particularly used for St. Peter, St. Philip, and St. Helen. The Eastern Orthodox churches often add another bar for the feet, slanting in reminiscence of St. Andrew, who is said to have introduced Christianity into Russia and to have been martyred on an X cross. A pope alone is seen with a cross with three upper bars.

A hand is the most frequently used symbol of God the Father, though an eye, a star, or rays of light are also seen. When the hand is used, the palm is extended downward and the fingers are arranged in the traditional position of blessing. In Latin lands the two forefingers are extended, the fourth and fifth being folded up. In Greek usage the forefinger is straight, the second finger slightly curved, and the thumb bends over the fourth and fifth fingers to form the sign of the cross. There are only two real symbols of the Holy Spirit: the dove, which is generally shown in descending flight, either the head or the whole body being surrounded with a tri-radiant nimbus or aureole; and the tongue of fire. The triangle, with the point either up or down, the trefoil—shamrock design, the triangle with three interlacing circles, and the fleur-de-lis—or lily design, are emblems of the Trinity. The fleur-de-lis is often seen on pew ends in Gothic churches, especially in the choirs.

An interesting design noted frequently in medieval glassware is a triangle with convex sides, a circle at each angle and another circle in the middle, the center circle being connected with the outer circles—as the outer circles are with one another—by double lines. The center circle stands for God, the outer circles for the

Father, Son, and Holy Spirit. Sometimes words are lettered on the connecting lines, an *est* (*is*) connecting each of the three outer circles with the inner circles, stating that the Father *is* God, the Son *is* God, the Holy Spirit *is* God; and a *non est* connecting each outer circle, stating that the Father *is not* the Son, the Son *is not* the Holy Spirit, the Holy Spirit *is not* the Father. Such mathematical theology delighted the minds of the scholastics. The device is being reintroduced today in some of the more philosophically minded of our Protestant groups.

From time immemorial the figures of saints and holy persons, both in Christian art and in pre-Christian art, have often been emphasized by a *glory, nimbus,* or *aureole* emanating from them. Though the glory is the more general term—properly including all the others—authors and artists use the words with varying meanings. Usually the aureole is the irradiation which surrounds the whole figure, generally of God the Father or the Son, or of a saint in his ascent to heaven. The nimbus surrounds the head, there being many different forms of it. A tri-radiant, or cruciform, nimbus is used only for divinity but a comparatively few nimbuses, for God the Father, are triangular. Some, especially in the East, are embellished with monograms in the angles. Saints' nimbuses are of various kinds: double-circled, radiant, crescent, or even square. Mottoes or texts are often written upon them. *Halo* is a term used more by laymen than by art historians. It is a circular nimbus.

Other symbols frequently seen in Christian art are the peacock for pride; the palm, sword, lance, axe, club, or wheel for martyrdom; fire for fervor; the banner for victory; the ship for the Church; the anchor for hope and security; the chalice, or clusters of wheat or grapes, for the Eucharist; the olive for peace; the lily for purity, and particularly as an emblem of the Virgin Mary; the apple for the fall of man; the pomegranate for immortality (on account of its many seeds); the skull for penance, especially in pictures of St. Francis; the dragon or serpent for Satan; and the quatrefoil for the four Gospels.

Candles are frequently used for symbolic purposes. In liturgical churches they must be made of unbleached beeswax. Light dispels darkness. It moves with miraculous speed. It gives warmth and nourishment to all of life. Originally, no doubt, candles and lamps were used largely for practical purposes, but they could hardly avoid symbolic attachments. In the early and medieval Church one pure white candle, called the paschal candle and placed in a stick near the altar upon the floor, symbolized the risen Christ. The paschal candle is still used in paschal season in some churches. Before churches were lighted by the easy means now at our disposal, this candle often assumed huge proportions. Churches today generally seem to prefer two candles, in separate sticks, either on the table or altar or near it, symbolizing the two natures of Christ, human and divine. In addition to these two, which are lighted at every service, it may seem advisable to employ one or two large Eucharistic candles when communion is celebrated. These might well stand in long sticks upon the floor. When a simple table is used, around which the minister and deacons or elders cluster, and upon which considerable numbers of plates of bread and trays of individual glasses are placed, table candles—like a standing cross—may prove to be decidedly in the way. For Protestants, of course, neither table candles nor Eucharistic candles are necessary. If candles are lighted on the empty table in non-communion services, their absence on communion Sundays would doubtless be noticed and regretted by many persons. Floor candles, lighted only for communion services, standing at the two ends of the table or up against the wall flanking the hanging cross, would seem therefore the best to use on such Sundays. In any case more than these four candles are ordinarily superfluous and have no particular significance in the usual Protestant service, though there are special services where their symbolism is specific and of great effectiveness.

In Orthodox churches, double- and triple-branched candlesticks are used at pontifical services, the bishop bestowing his blessing upon the faithful with them. A seven-branched candlestick is often stationed behind the altar, and is used in processions. Two tapers are also placed upon the altar. In the Roman Catholic church, two candles are used at a priest's low Mass; four at a pontifical (bishop's) low Mass; six at a priest's high Mass; and at a Mass offered before the exposed Sacrament, twelve candles. A candle is placed in the hand of a candidate at the time of his baptism and often also in the hand of one dying. A votive candle is one which is lighted before a shrine or statue to mark the fulfillment of a vow. The seven-branched candlestick of the Jews is used by Christians to denote the seven churches of the Revelation, the seven sacraments, or the seven virtues or gifts of the Holy Spirit. The three-branched candlestick is an emblem of the Trinity. The candlestick itself, as apart from the candle, is emblematic of the Church, as the agency which, though it does not have light of itself, yet holds forth the light of Christ.

The church building contains many architectural symbols. The center aisle is an emblem of the march of life, reaching from the baptismal font at the door to the altar in the sanctuary. The pillars signify the apostles and saints while the pews speak of the living worshipers in the ongoing Church. The entrance end of the building is known as the "west end"; and the head end as the "east end," in recollection of the fact that Jesus is the "Sun of Righteousness," ever rising and nevermore going down. During service the Gospel is read from the "north" (or Gospel) side of the altar, and the Epistle from the "south" (or Epistle) side. These terms are often used even if the church does not face toward the east.

Where there are three steps they symbolize the Trinity. Seven is the number of perfection. It speaks of entrance into heaven, and again of the seven virtues or of the seven arts. Twelve is the number of the minor prophets and of the apostles; thus there are often twelve pillars. Over the outer central portal of a Gothic church the Last Judgment has often been sculptured as the most important fact of a Christian's life. On the south side are Christ and the Gospels; on the north, an Old Testament scene. Thus we see that the honor position on the outside of a church is the south side; on the inside, especially in the chancel itself, it is the north. Inside everything is oriented from the viewpoint of the altar. The Gospel side is on the right side of the altar as the altar faces the people but, outside of the church, the Gospel side is at the right of the people as the people face the church.

To an initiated worshiper this symbolism contains much of power and significance. Keeping eyes and minds open for symbolism in the glasswork, woodwork, metalwork, fabrics, books, pictures, and statues, and in the fundamental architecture itself, is not only increasing aesthetic delight but—what is vastly more important—broadening the avenues of spiritual expression. Although some people are left cold by symbols, and although it is hardly to be expected that Protestants in general will use more than a small proportion of those mentioned in this survey, we should nevertheless be careful that nothing is employed or arranged in our buildings in such a way as to hurt the sensibilities of those who do know and appreciate their historic meaning. If possible the style and type of furniture should be chosen by the pastor, the church committee, and the architect, working together. Every church, no matter how small, should have a continuing art committee and consulting architect to pass upon all furnishings, monuments, decorations, or symbols. Much heartache will be spared our descendants if we follow this simple prudence.

Table, Altar, and Silver

IT HAS ALREADY been suggested that a table is better than a solid altar in the center of the chancel. Since the cross should be plainly visible as the chief symbol of sacrifice, the presence of an altar would only duplicate this symbolism. A table indicates fellowship. Table and cross together express our faith both in sacrifice and in fellowship. These words advocating a table rather than an altar are not written without a pang. To some the altar is indeed the Church itself, the very throne of God; and we all hesitate to lose the beauty and the power of this age-old association and belief. Furthermore, we realize that, just as the sacrificial qualities of an altar reside in a table—it was upon a table that the Bread was broken and the Wine poured forth— so the communion qualities of a table reside in an altar for sacrifice most surely implies fellowship. The writer therefore has no quarrel with those who prefer to use the term "altar table." But to him it still seems clear that the early Protestants were right in restoring the pre-eminence of the table aspect; for in the early Church, as in the Upper Room, it *was* a table. The mistake of the reformers was that in their great effort to be primitive, they also abolished the symbol of the cross. Table and cross are both needed to bring out the full meaning of both the Supper and Calvary.

The table should be treated with respect, not for what it is but for what it symbolizes. Only those things should be placed upon it as rest naturally upon a table. On Sundays when the Lord's Supper is not celebrated, flowers, candlesticks, possibly a chalice, and if desired, offering plates, are suitable—nothing else. The middle of the table, unless there is a chalice, should be left empty, the flowers and candlesticks being at either end. This arrangement will lift the eyes of the worshipers to the cross hanging upon the end wall. On the table it would seem sufficient to have either flowers or candles, not both, unless the table is large enough to hold both without crowding. If the table is short it would be better to place the candles upon it, and the flowers on small tables or stands flanking it. In addition to these table candles, there may, whenever communion is celebrated, also be two eucharistic candles, which may well stand in long sticks resting upon the floor. On communion Sundays the table should be covered with a white linen cloth and furnished with the proper utensils.

If an altar is used, the same care for fitness should be taken. On an altar a standing cross is quite in keeping; this may be placed either upon the altar itself or upon a retable behind it. Traditionally, the altar-top, or mensa, in liturgical churches, has five incised Greek crosses, the largest being in the center. An altar ordinarily has three coverings: one simple linen undercloth the exact size of the mensa; one cloth with a superfrontal attached, hanging down over the front of the altar for a distance of several inches or more; and on top of these another cloth, called the "fair linen," which is the exact width of the mensa but which hangs over the two ends of the altar, sometimes almost to the floor. This fair linen cloth is generally embroidered with five crosses in white. Sometimes there is also a frontal, covering the whole front of the altar, hanging from under the superfrontal and reaching the floor. Upon the altar, in addition to the cross, are often a Bible or Gospel, a service book, and at least two candles. In the absence of a frontal, an altar is sometimes carved or inlaid with some suitable Christian emblem—a vine and wheat design; a ship, representing the Church; an anchor; a cross; a cross with crown; a crown of thorns; or some other carved representation suitable to the idea of sacrifice.

Leaf of Ivory Diptych, probably English, fifteenth century: showing scenes from the Passion of Christ. (*Courtesy of the Metropolitan Museum of Art, New York*)

Portal of St. Trophimus, Arles, France, a twelfth century, Romanesque gateway.
The tympanum contains Christ as Judge, with the symbols of the four Evangelists.
The statues, the columns and capitals, the iron work on the doors, and many other
details are worth careful study. They all help to build up an emotional as well as an
intellectual attitude toward the Church, and contribute greatly to the expression of
Christian ideals. (*Courtesy of the Avery Library, Columbia University*)

RIGHT. John Constable (English) 1776–1837: Salisbury Cathedral from the Bishop's Garden; Detail of the Transept. Note the characteristic Gothic buttresses and pointed arches. (*Courtesy of the Frick Collection, New York*)

BELOW. Cathedral of St. Sophia, Kiev, Russia. Much of the light comes from windows in the domes. From *L'architecture Religieuse Russe*, by G. K. Loukomski, published by Leroux, Paris. (*Courtesy of the Avery Library, Columbia University*)

Washington Cathedral, Fuller Memorial; Wrought-Iron Screen by Samuel Yellin.
Note the hanging banners which soften yet add color and warmth to the masonry.

Cathedral of the Dormition (also known as the Cathedral of the Assumption), Moscow; altar end, with iconostasis and icons. Note the cross with three crossbars over the candelabra at the right. From *L'architecture Religieuse Russe,* by G. K. Loukomski, published by Leroux, Paris. (*Courtesy of the Avery Library Columbia University*)

TOP. Christ Church, Episcopal, South Hamilton, Massachusetts. The cock is an ancient symbol, entirely suitable for a church steeple. (*Courtesy of the Reverend Angus Dun, Jr.*)

BOTTOM. St. Paul's Episcopal Church, Kansas City, Missouri. The large and almost empty table is impressive. There is a design of grapes, trefoils, and quatrefoils in the wrought-iron altar rail. Note the credence board and the interesting arrangement of candles. (*Courtesy of Samuel Yellin*)

St. Mark's Roman Catholic Church, Burlington, Vermont; a colorful, simple, and dignified modern building, in true functional style, with a natural setting of tall trees lending height. (*Courtesy of the Reverend William A. Tennien*)

The Altar and Sanctuary, St. Mark's Church, Burlington. The altar is entirely surrounded by a railing. Its central placement and table-like form indicate a new movement among Roman Catholics. The simplicity and dignity of crucifix, table, and furniture appeal to Protestants and Catholics alike. (*Courtesy of the Reverend William A. Tennien*)

The Bruton Parish Church, Williamsburg, Virginia. (*Courtesy of the Reverend Mr. Craighill, Rector*)

First Congregational Church, Southington, Connecticut. Greek revival façade, built in 1828. The bulletin board seeks to be in keeping with the style of the church. (*Photograph by Lincoln Wade Barnes*)

The Chapel and School of Religion, Yenching University, Peiping, China. The color is buff, with red columns and window frames and multicolored eaves.

Pilgrim Congregational Church, St. Louis, Missouri; window in the pastor's study. From the cross and from the four Gospels falls the seed of the word. At the left it drops upon stony ground, birds eat it, thorns choke it, and it grows feebly and in confusion. At the right, the seed finds good soil where it produces abundant harvest, upright and straight. The border design includes three-fold leaves, symbolic of the Trinity and of growth. The Dove represents the Holy Spirit, and the stars, hope and light. The lettering is characteristic of Mr. Frei's work. (*Designed and made by Emil Frei*)

St. Vincent's Archabbey, crypt, Latrobe, Pennsylvania. Stained glass window in black and white, in memory of the Benedictine Peter the Venerable. A ray of light shines from the *Chi Rho* upon three praying monks. The phases of the sun and moon indicate the necessity of the regularity of prayer. Designed and made by Emil Frei and Robert Harmon. (*Courtesy of the Reverend Quentin Schaut, O.S.B.*)

Princeton University Chapel. The Great East Window, called the "Love Window," symbolizing Jesus' words, "A new commandment I give unto you, that ye love one another as I have loved you." (*Designed and made by Charles J. Connick, 1928*)

Flemish Tapestry, of about 1510: "The Procession to Calvary." An excellent example of mural design with partial perspective, warm colors, and balanced pattern. (*Courtesy of the William Rockhill Nelson Gallery of Art, Kansas City*)

OPPOSITE PAGE

UPPER LEFT. Congregational Church, Newton Center, Massachusetts. Communion table, standing out from wall, with hanging cross and eucharistic candles. Symbols of the Trinity, Christ, the Holy Spirit, and the Four Evangelists surmount the reredos; on the table itself are the *Chi Rho* with *Alpha* and *Omega*, the wheat, and the chalice. (*Photograph: John R. Scotford*)

UPPER RIGHT. Congregational Church, Kalamazoo, Michigan. Chancel, with rood screen, I N R I below the rood cross, fleur-de-lis designs, and the Beatitudes in suitable Gothic letters beside a splendid window. (*Photograph: John R. Scotford*)

LOWER LEFT. Second Church in Newton, West Newton, Massachusetts. Baptismal record book and case. The carved angels are brightly painted on both sides. (*Photograph: John R. Scotford*)

LOWER RIGHT. Children's Chapel in the Second Church in Newton. The window is of Christ and the children, flanked by angels, with the angel motif carried on in the wood carving below. (*Photograph: John R. Scotford*)

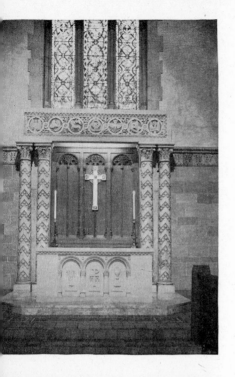

LEFT. University of Pittsburgh, Heinz Memorial Chapel. Wrought-Iron Lamp by Samuel Yellin.

BELOW. Washington Cathedral: Wrought-Iron Ring Handle and Escutcheon in the Chapel of St. Joseph of Arimathea, by Samuel Yellin.

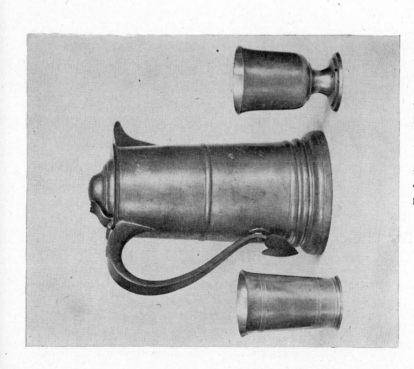

LEFT. Early American Ecclesiastical Pewter. (Courtesy of Mr. and Mrs. Henry B. Reardon, Jr.)

RIGHT. Gothic Chalice from the workshop of Holger Rasmussen, Copenhagen, Denmark. Note the two forms of the *Chi Rho*, the lower one also including the *Alpha* and *Omega*. (*Courtesy of the St. Bernward Guild, New York*)

Congregational Church, Fox-
boro, Massachusetts, St. Francis
Sanctuary Garden. (*Photograph: John R. Scotford*)

Washington Cathedral:
The Bishop's Garden.
Wrought-iron gates by
Samuel Yellin.

In the early Church the only book allowed upon the altar was the Gospel book. At present service books are often seen; and sometimes still, the Bible. This is quite acceptable if these books are read by the pastor facing the altar, as in liturgical churches. In free churches it would seem better to have only one Bible for pastoral use, and that upon its natural receptacle, the lectern. Standing upon an altar, opened toward a congregation, and un-read even by the minister, a Bible gives a pathetical appearance of uselessness; and the symbolism of having the Word at the foot of the Cross is not either meaningful or inspiring.

Behind the altar, a reredos of wood or stone or a dossal curtain are alike suitable. Whether the curtain is figured or free of design, it is usually more pleasing for it to hang in loose folds. Whatever design there is should contain symbols suitable to Christian usage. It is perhaps unnecessary to add that the altar or table should always be of good, strong material, sound in craftsmanship, and that the design should be such as to make it almost an architectural part of the building. Whether altar or table, it should be as large as the setting can afford, and should stand on the highest level of the chancel, clear of all other furniture so that it may dominate its surroundings. Beware of the common fault of partially hiding the altar by an overlarge pulpit or lectern.

Silver used for communion is bound to be expensive; and so, while a church is making its purchase, it might just as well spend enough in the first place really to express the deep devotion which we all feel when attending the table of our Lord. Good silver-ware need not and should not be ornate. Although in many churches hygiene has directed that the wine be distributed by means of individual glasses or by intinction, nevertheless there ought to be a chalice also, standing upon the middle of the table. The pastor, and perhaps the deacons, could use this chalice; its symbolism is reminiscent, for until recently it was practically universal. The plates for the bread should be matched, in their design, to the chalice; and the napkins to the fair linen table-cloth. It may be interesting in connection with this discussion of table silver to recall that Jacob Boehme, the great seventeenth-century mystic, reached the turning point of his life when his eye happened to fall upon a polished pewter bowl. Its gleam and grace became the agents for bringing his soul into a vivid experience of God.

The offering plates need not be placed upon the table and never should be there on communion Sundays. They may be kept upon a stand at the entrance end of the church until after the offering has been collected. Then, with the offerings in them, they may be brought down the aisle by the ushers, held before the cross while the prayer or chant of dedication is being made, and then either placed upon the table or carried to one side of the chancel where a special small table stands prepared for their reception. The procedure may be the same whether a table or an altar is used and whether it is in a chancel or in front of the pulpit.

Flowers, Flags, and Hangings

THE ARRANGEMENT of flowers is more important than most people would imagine. Their presence in a church has a threefold purpose: to stand as a symbol of God's creative handiwork in nature; to express the mood of the worshipers, particularly in respect to the season of year and its accompanying feelings; and to call attention, by their placement, to the central symbols of our worship.

The color of the flowers should follow in part the church year and in part the seasonal year. Christmas is the natural time for red and green; Lent and Easter for white; Whitsunday for red; Thanksgiving for yellow. Don't let us overdo the matter; nature itself is generally a sufficient guide to color scheme. Above all let us avoid sentimental efforts, such as red, white, and blue flowers for a patriotic holiday. An arrangement which calls attention to itself in such a bizarre fashion detracts from the mood of wonder at God's handiwork. The canon of simplicity here as always should be kept in mind. Never should the table be pushed about to make an effective stand for a flower exhibit. Never should a church be "trimmed" simply for display, whether it be at Christmas, a wedding, a funeral, or any other occasion. Profuse employment of greens or flowers, provided they are dignified in their arrangement, massed in the proper proportions, and centered toward the cross and table or altar, is by no means out of place. It is not the number of flowers or the size of the bouquets, nor even, ordinarily, their color, but rather their arrangement, that counts. Their purpose is to aid in the worship of God. The more they seem to be built into the church as an architect himself would place them, the better. At every church wedding, consultation ought to be held with the flower committee of the church to make certain that proper worship procedure is not upset.

Flags also are items which many people find it difficult to dispose in church. A flag in church should have but one purpose—to express the Christian feeling of worship. A national flag, therefore, should never be displayed in church either for the purpose of decorating the church or for the purpose of honoring the flag. We come to church to honor God and God alone. The flag stands for the nation and in church it stands for the nation at prayer. It should be in a position subordinate to, and possibly inclined toward, the cross. Whether it be in the chancel or out of the chancel is immaterial. Insofar as it does not violate the purposes of church worship, there is no reason why it should not conform to the rules of any patriotic organization. It must never be in such a place as to call attention to itself as such, or where it cries out for precedence or protocol. The nation cannot be vainglorious or dare to set itself up as a rival of God.

Other flags should be treated in the same way. United Nations flags, state flags, and church flags may all properly be present, as well as flags or banners of the Sunday school, Christian Endeavor, or other Christian societies, particularly on special Sundays. In church it would seem to be unnecessary to have a symbol of the Church. If a church flag is desired there is no real objection to it, provided the guiding principles are remembered. The church flag stands for the Christian community, and in church it stands for this community at prayer. Like the national flag it should therefore defer to the cross. There need be no clash of opinion about whether the church flag or the national flag is to take precedence; such a clash would be most unseemly among Christian people. How many times did Jesus have to rebuke those who would strive for priority of position! Let the people who believe that the Church is greater than the nation nevertheless give way to the others out of purity and humility of heart, if the others persist in desiring them to do so. Though there be no clash of loyalties but only an earnest wish to arrange the matter in the best way, then it would seem that the position of honor might very well be alternated between the two. In cases where emotions are unduly aroused, perhaps the best way out of the difficulty is not to have either flag; or if the national flag is demanded, not to have the church flag. Or again it is possible to have the national and the state flags only, a choice of symbols which brings no opposition of opinions. Let the national flag then have the place of honor, but let them both be subordinate to the cross, thus calling attention to the one really central symbol.

Tapestries, wall banners, or other hangings may be used to excellent purpose, particularly in stone Gothic churches. They originally had the function of reducing the cold in the draughty buildings of Northern Europe and even now they give forth a feeling of comfort which relieves our shivering reactions to stony texture or color. Flanders, France, Lower Germany, and England were the homes of most of the tapestries of the Middle Ages. Being made especially for high walls, the best medieval tapestries have a flatness and a lack of perspective which the more naturalistic Renaissance scorned. We are coming now to see, once again, that tapestries, like stained glass, are not to be employed for the purpose of edification but as conductors for the expression of the human desire for consolation and warmth. Their designs should therefore not be obstrusively representational nor contrived to call attention to themselves.

Fonts

EXCEPT AMONG THOSE who practice immersion, the font is usually not in the chancel or on the platform. Often it is in the narthex, just inside the west door, signifying that this is the first step of the newcomer into the Church. At other times it is in one of the transepts. Or again it is on the main floor of the church just before the chancel but toward one side. That the font should be excluded from the chancel is right, as the chancel is the sign of the redeemed life, and the newly baptized person is just a beginner in Christian living. Yet to have it nestle close to the chancel is also right and gives a feeling of comfort to the new Christian or his sponsors. Furthermore, the ceremony of baptism can then be a part of the Sunday service of plenary worship and not a mere private affair for child and family only, as it must nearly always be if the font is in the narthex or at the entrance end of the nave.

Some basins are circular in their shape, some are square but the majority are octagonal. The reason for eight sides is that eight is the number for regeneration. Such symbolism is somewhat obscure; we need not hold meticulously to it. However, other things being equal, there is a certain amount of value in staying in the traditional line. Of course it is not necessary to have a font at all. A simple bowl, held by a deacon, is sufficient and in many ways is even better.

Color

IN FURNISHING the church, proper judgment about color is a very desirable and even necessary matter. Colors have real emotional associations. Red startles us—it stands for the sun, fire, blood, passion, danger, power. Green, on the other hand, gives a pleasant sense of well-being—it signifies peace, progress, growth, life, plenty. Blue is for the eternal heavens—wisdom, truth, faith, loyalty, dignity. The warm colors—red, yellow, orange, and gold—seem to be always advancing toward us. On the other hand, the cool colors—green, blue, and their derivatives—give an impression of withdrawal. The neutrals—gray, brown, buff, green, and pastel shades—express calmness and rest. Cool or neutral colors would therefore seem to be the best for the general background tones of the walls, carpets, seats, cushions, and woodwork. Much would depend, to be sure, upon the architectural style of the church; but in any case neither a glaring white, nor a warm color, should be the prevailing tone of the nave. This coolness and balm will be relieved by the warmth of emotion which comes from stained-glass windows, or else the glimpses of nature's blues and greens through the clear glass of a Georgian building.

It is in the chancel that the massing of the primary colors takes place. The chancel is where all eyes should be focused. With light and color as well as action concentrated here, it ought to be easy for people to unite their emotional experiences in its view. Except for the windows, therefore, which cast a general colorful tone over the whole interior, the moving, stimulating, vibrating hues are all gathered in the place where the imaginations of the people are living. In the nave let us keep color inconspicuous. In the chancel let it be in lively evidence.

Although the fair linen cloth of the altar is always white, the frontal and superfrontal may change with the seasons. So also may the dossal curtains, the vestments of the priests or ministers, the bookmarks for the Bible, and the other cloths or hangings that are used in the chancel. Only the richest churches can indulge in such grandeur but even an average church may have several differently colored dossal curtains, bookmarks, and stoles.

Traditionally, white is the color of the festivals of our Lord, of the Virgin, of the angels, and of the saints who were not martyrs. Red is used on Whitsunday, signifying the tongues of fire, and on martyrs' days. Purple or violet, being expressive of penitence, are for Lent and Advent. Black is only for Good Friday or funeral services. Green is used at all other times, and especially in Trinity season, following Whitsunday. These are the five liturgical colors. They need not be followed with slavish obedience. Individual churches are quite capable of working out schemes which seem to suit their needs and purses. For an ordinary church not overburdened with money, three colors may be suggested: red, purple, and green. Red might be used at Christmas and Epiphany, Whitsunday, All-Saints' Day, or other saints' festivals, and on communion Sunday. Let the red be crimson or maroon rather than scarlet. Purple or violet could be employed during Lent and Advent or, if preferred, during Lent alone. Advent, for free churchmen, is losing its penitential significance and speaks rather of preparation for the coming joy of Christmas; hence red might seem to some to be more appropriate for Advent than purple. For the rest of the year, green, denoting energy, life, and growth, is in all probability the best color to employ. Even this simple variety will be found a stimulus to worship.

Costuming is an ancient and a high art. The liturgical churches have strict rules and rubrics covering vestments, into which we need not go. In the free churches the matter is usually left to the individual minister or music committee.

Some ministers and choirs still persist in wearing ordinary business or social clothing in church, as in the "world." They insist that since they are not priests, they should therefore not attempt to set themselves off from the laity. In other churches though the choirs are robed the minister still maintains the common touch by wearing street garb. Generally now both choirs and ministers are gowned, the minister in a so-called Geneva scholar's robe, and the choirs either in the same fashion or in gowns and surplices. Mortarboard hats or skullcaps are sometimes worn by women due to a strange reverence for a certain passage in which St. Paul said that women ought not to appear in church uncovered.

The present writer prefers colored gowns for choirs—maroon, blue, or dark green—covered by fairly long surplices of white. The white thus predominating, the same gowns can be worn, if desired, at all seasons. Of all colors black seems to be the least suitable for the natural moods of Christians, and there is little excuse for its present popularity. As for the minister, let him wear a black Genevan gown only if his congregation is insistent, for black inculcates gloom. At a funeral, perhaps, people might prefer him to wear black; yet even there Christian faith, hope, and joy should serve to prevent it. To the Christian even Good Friday is an anticipation of triumph.

It might be acceptable, therefore, for the minister to wear a red garment when the season calls for red, green when it calls for green, purple when it calls for purple. If the church can afford but one set of garments for its minister, maroon seems to be as good a color as any. Over his gown or cassock he may wear a surplice, three-quarter length, flowing, with wide sleeves. And over the surplice a stole, with very simple embroidery at the ends, in the proper seasonal color. Stoles are only for ministers, priests, or ordained deacons; they are not properly worn by choirs. For ages long this custom of reserving the stole for ordained men has been continued and it is not needful for us now to change it. A stole signifies both the yoke under which the clergyman serves and also the kerchief with which he wipes the sweat from his brow. If a minister desires he may wear white bands at the neck; but in any case let the neck of the gown be high enough to cover his tie. Academic hoods are not usually in place in a service of worship, since they call attention to personal intellectual honors and attainments rather than to ministerial status.

Woodwork and Metalwork

THE WOODWORK and metalwork of a church, as shown in the pulpit, choir stalls, prayer benches, railings, pews, screens, hymn boards, memorials, lighting fixtures, and other fittings, should always be in keeping, both in style and in color, with the church as a whole. It is perhaps necessary to emphasize the fact that the style of hymn boards and memorial tablets and the lettering thereon should also be harmonious with the whole. Many seem to think that Gothic letters are more churchly than any other style but this is true, of course, only in Gothic churches. Hymn boards, with tattered, dirty, and unmatched figures, seem to invite the congregation to stay away from God almost as frequently as they do to draw near in an experience of soul-releasing song. When calendars are used, hymn boards are not necessary.

Wood carving is a useful addition to almost any church if it is practiced with restraint and propriety. A Gothic building calls for elaboration of carving on altar, reredos, choir screen, stalls, pulpit, lectern, pew ends and perhaps elsewhere. Such carving may be a powerful means of emotional release. Statues on the altar fronts or organ screens often induce a soaring spirit. In a Romanesque, Georgian, or modernistic building, such carving should be kept within chaste limits if used at all. Fluting and slightly ornamented capitals are generally sufficient to add gayety or relief to the sternness of colonial buildings. A low interior, with saucer dome, and horizontal lines of galleries enclosing three sides, almost demands such fluting to give upward urge to human feelings. Metalwork in altar furnishings, lamps and chandeliers, railings, gates, doorknobs and knockers, gives another opportunity to symbolize Christian faith and ideals. The danger in both woodwork and metalwork is that the temptation to overelaboration will not be overcome. Only that which is needed for use, or helpful to a sense of mystery and worship, should be admitted.

Words to the Wise

BEFORE CLOSING this chapter it may not be out of place to add two words of warning. The first word is against being caught in the fascination of minutiae. There is a real danger here. Some there are who become so annoyed over being confronted by what they think is the wrong number of candles, or a table a little too high or too short, or a bouquet of flowers not well enough arranged, or a tawdry stained-glass window, or the flatting of a high F by the soprano section, or an unfortunate elocutionary habit on the part of the minister, that they lose the spirit of worship. Let the leaders seek ever to make all arrangements as suitable and harmonious as possible but let the worshipers nevertheless be tolerant of mistakes or poor taste. To allow one's self to come to the point where worship cannot be satisfying without a particular symbol or arrangement or method or order of service is to court idolatry. Some kind of form is unavoidable but correct form, while we must ever strive to attain it, eludes definition and can therefore never be essential.

The other word of warning is against narrow group-mindedness. Although we naturally become accustomed to our own way, our own prayer book, our own type of music, our own denominational mores, let us make definite efforts to express ourselves in other manners also. It is a good thing for an Episcopalian to attend a Quaker meeting from time to time, or a Lutheran, a Baptist, or a Congregationalist a Roman Catholic, or a Methodist a Hebrew synagogue, or a Unitarian a Pentacostal meeting in a rented store. On these occasions attend not merely to observe but to enter into the services in fullest sympathy and social expression. That there is not just one correct way to worship God some Christians need to be constantly reminding themselves. If you explain to your own minister what you are doing, the chances are very strong that he will be neither shocked nor jealous, but rather enthusiastic. Until the day of the universal church, tolerance and understanding are called for. There is no better method of hastening the day than to make ourselves at home in all the various arts by which different groups of Christians, with sincerity and joy, worship the same God.

CHAPTER V

The Art of Music

MUSIC, NEXT TO conversation, is probably the most common of the arts. Practically everyone is a musician of some sort or other. Furthermore, it is also safe to say that music is used in churches more than in any other institution. Practically every Christian, at least every Protestant Christian, sings. Even in India, China, and other lands where group singing had never been practiced until it was introduced by Christianity, hymns are now a universal means of Protestant worship.

A story is told of a group of Christian college students in China on their way to a "retreat" in the hills near Peking, singing hymns as they marched along. An old-fashioned Chinese village scholar stood astounded by the roadside and watched the intelligent-looking, eager-eyed, thoroughly Chinese group go by singing. He stopped the last member of the party and asked him who they were and what they were up to.

"We are Christian students going to a conference," was the reply.

"But why are you singing? And what are you singing about?"

"We are singing because we are Christian. We are singing forth our Good News, because we believe in it so earnestly we cannot help but sing it."

"Well," replied the astonished old scholar, "this is something new under the sun! I must look into this Christianity; I must look into it!"

In the West, Christians have no monopoly on singing. Indeed music originated centuries before the Church was born. By some students music is even considered to be a more ancient mode of human expression than speech. The Indians and Chinese also used music, though not in vocal groups, as far back as history has any records. So also did the Chaldeans, Egyptians, Hebrews, various tribes of Africans, Greeks, Celts, Slavs, and Germans. And all of these peoples engaged in it at least partly as a form of religious expression. All Greek plays contained singing: the word "chorus" comes from the group of dancers who sang and danced in a circle, in the Greek dramas. "Choir" and "carol" are derivatives of "chorus." Our Western music is largely a heritage from the Eastern Mediterranean peoples.

In the Days of the Bible

THE HEBREWS, we know from the many references in the Old Testament, were frequent and enthusiastic singers and players. Music was used both in Temple and in synagogue worship. Singing, dancing, and instrumental playing were accepted methods of social religious utterance. The Old Testament mentions many kinds of instruments: drums, pipes, percussives of various sorts, and stringed instruments. They were played both in orchestra and singly, both for religious and also for non-religious purposes. Vocal music, though there is no evidence of harmony, was used both in solo and in unison. There were huge choirs of professional "singing men and singing women." (II Samuel 19:35, II Chronicles 5:13, etc.) The Psalms were written to music and were sung antiphonally in services. There are many directions for the singers and accompanists in the Psalms.

Certain passages in Deuteronomy, the Prophets, and other books were doubtless meant to be sung. Even prayers were set to music. (Habakkuk 3:1) The Jews were, as they still are, very musical. Perhaps it was because they were discouraged from painting and sculpture by their fear of idolatry that they were thereby led to concentrate upon their literature and their music. The chief reason why they loved music was probably that they were religious, for music is a most natural manifestation of social religious experiences.

The earliest Christians were, as we know, greatly influenced by the Hebrews in their whole system of worship; hence they naturally fell heir to the Hebrew musical tradition. Although there is but little reference to music in the New Testament, we are informed that Jesus and his disciples sang a hymn at the last supper. (Mark 14:26) This was possibly the "Hallel" or Hallelujah Psalms (113–118), commonly used at the time of the Passover. "Hallelujah," meaning "Praise God," introduced many of the Psalms, and is used in the Book of Revelation in its Greek form, "Alleluia." The opening chapters of Luke have also preserved for us a number of Messianic hymns which undoubtedly sprang into use soon after the death of Jesus. St. Paul instructed the Christians to teach and admonish one another in "psalms and hymns and spiritual songs, singing with grace in your hearts to the Lord." (Colossians 3:16) Several early hymns were included by St. Paul in his letters (Ephesians 5:14; Philippians 2:6–11, etc.) And the author of Revelation quoted a number of songs of praise.

Early and Medieval Times

DURING THE SECOND and third centuries, due partly to persecutions which often necessitated secret and silent meetings, music in the Church declined but it never entirely died out. When Christianity became legal under Constantine the songs burst forth again in shouts of joy. It is difficult for us to reconstruct these ancient melodies, though studies are proceeding which some day may bring better results. A few stone and papyrus fragments have been uncovered, giving us notations of Greek music according to an alphabetical system; and some students have thought that they have observed similarities between these Greek compositions and early medieval Christian chants. It may be deduced from this that much of the early church music was not dissimilar from the plainsong chants of the sixth and seventh centuries. St. Ambrose (340–397), Bishop of Milan, forged an important link between Eastern and Western music. He collected and arranged ancient hymns, largely from Antioch, established a choir school, encouraged antiphonal singing and the singing of hymns, and sought to reduce all of church music to a unified system.

Pope Gregory the Great (540–604) is one of the best known of all Christian saints. It was he who, among other important accomplishments, sent the first Italian missionaries to England. He also, in his busy life, insisted upon and gave much of his time to the cultivation of good music in the Church. Though not himself a great musician, he established a school of church singing and exerted a larger influence over this field of art than any other person before the Reformation. Gregorian music was not original either with Gregory or with his age. It was a development of Greek music, through the Ambrosian, marked by exalted Christian idealism. Because Gregory urged upon the musicians of his day the necessity of refining and organizing this plainsong style, his name is forever attached to it.

Gregorian chanting is, in the minds of its devotees, the purest and most religious music yet produced in the Western world. It follows a mode neither major nor minor; that is, it has a scale different from those to which we are accustomed. It is slow in its motion, without measured beats, non-chromatic, non-harmonic, and comparatively narrow in its range. It is intended for choir singing, the boys or tenors at times carrying the air while the men or basses follow an octave lower. This is true *a cappella* music; that is, singing without instrumental accompaniment *from the chancel*. Such singing was developed at a time when large churches were being built and is especially suitable to them, the haunting melodies roaming amidst the arches and transepts and forming harmonies by their echoes. The effect upon us today is strange and foreign but the more we hear it the more are we likely to fall under its powerful spell. Resonant, severely simple, yet gloriously rich in its variations, it lifts both singers and listeners toward heaven.

There has been a marked revival of interest in plainsong chants in our age, principally among the Roman Catholics but also among Lutherans, Anglicans, American Episcopalians, and even some of the larger free churches. In the new Episcopal hymnal there are no fewer than thirty-seven such tunes for congregational singing. They can best be introduced to a group which does not know them through the phonograph recordings of the chapel music of the monastery of Solesmes. Let anyone who wishes to discover the glories of this medieval Christian expression visit the Trappist Priory of Our Lady of the Valley near Providence in Rhode Island, or some other monastery where such chanting is used, and attend the daily "hours." An experience of great beauty is in store for him.

The Renaissance

FOR ABOUT SIX hundred years plain song held sway in the Church. Then slowly, under the influence of the Renaissance, there dawned a new type of music, harmonic in form. About the same time as these first tentative experiments with harmony, the organ entered the Church, thus hastening the development of part singing. The first harmonic work came in a device called "organum," or the duplicate singing of the melody beginning at the dominant tone, generally a fourth below the tonic. The two parts were continued to the end of the song, producing an effect somewhat similar to much Russian music of today. From this it was but a natural step to four-part and even eight-part harmony. Thence derived counterpoint, or polyphony, in which there are independent melodies by the different parts, all harmonizing with one another.

Palestrina, who died in 1594, was the culminating genius of this polyphonic school, and one of the greatest composers of all time. He was saintly in his private life and worked entirely for the Church. Victoria in Spain, Schütz in Germany, Orlando de Lasso in the Netherlands, Tallis, Byrd and Orlando Gibbons in England, are other great Renaissance figures. Roman Catholic music was written almost entirely for the choir, mostly to give body to the responses and choruses of the Mass, and can therefore be used in our Protestant churches only in modified or excerpt form.

Tallis and Gibbons, however, became Anglicans, and also wrote psalms and hymns for congregational singing. Though few of their pieces are to be found in our modern books, they are beginning again deservedly to return to favor, both in America and even more in England. The music of this polyphonic school is highly intellectual and at the same time deeply expressive of Christian devotion. It goes best with its original Latin words with their long, resonant syllables. Unfortunately Palestrina is represented in many of our hymnals used today by only one composition: the Easter hymn, *The Strife Is O'er*. The most recent books are giving him more prominence. It is notable that the motion pictures, when they wish to employ a religious background, very often turn to Palestrina.

With the invention of printing, many of the medieval carols and folk songs were written down, standardized, and thus preserved. Some of the tunes had been religious songs from the very beginning. Others were adopted by the Church and turned into hymns. There were also a number of great Latin and Greek hymns—most of them in the Breviary and a few in the Mass book—which had been in the possession of the Church for centuries. Of these hymns the majority were known only by the priests, monks, and nuns.

The Reformation

BOTH THE ROMAN CATHOLIC and the Orthodox churches for many generations had kept music largely in the choir, the chanted congregational responses growing fewer and fewer as time went on. In most places these two historic churches also used ancient languages, unknown by the people, in their services.

Martin Luther was not only a revolutionist of the first rank but also a singer and a lover of music. With two strokes he changed the whole musical outlook of the Church: first, by returning the music to the people, where it had been in earliest times; and second, by putting the service into the native languages which the people could understand. Luther also wrote hymns of his own, both music and words, the greatest being *A Mighty Fortress Is Our God*. His tunes, from various sources including popular folk music, are in the slow-moving and powerful chorale form dear to the heart of everyone who ever learns them. This Lutheran release of song had a tremendous influence not only upon the Protestant movement but upon our whole Western civilization. Luther knew what every revolutionist and every evangelist and every missionary has since learned: that music is an important adjunct to any movement that would gain rapid popular support. There is an effort among Roman Catholics now to restore certain hymns to the people; in a few of their churches one will even find small hymnals in the pews.

Johann Sebastian Bach (1685–1750), following Luther by two hundred years, and a far more finished and prolific composer than Luther, brought the chorale form, as well as a number of other forms of musical composition, to its highest point. Like Palestrina, Bach was a devoted and saintly Christian. He was a Lutheran, a man of profound intellectual depth and breadth, and is often said to be the greatest of all the masters of music. The *Passion According to St. Matthew* and the *Mass in B Minor* are his finest choral works; many of his fugues and other compositions for the organ are also of magnificent power and beauty. More than any other composer, Bach gives expression to the best that is in the souls of millions of Christians in churches the world around. It is to the credit of our age that Bach, neglected for several generations, is now once again greatly loved and widely heard.

Mention must be made also of George Frederick Handel (1658–1759), who, though not strictly a church musician, nevertheless did write some compositions for the Church and much music that is thoroughly Christian in spirit. His "Messiah," composed like his oratorios for the concert stage, has nevertheless probably liberated more pure and exalted Christian enjoyment than any other similar piece of music in history. Following the example set by George II, listeners still rise, by popular consent, for *The Hallelujah Chorus*, a mark of respect not accorded to any other Christian composition. Handel wrote many oratorios, anthems, and *Te Deums*, portions of which are still often performed, the anthems and *Te Deums* having been composed specifically as church music.

From Puritans to Methodists

ANOTHER FLOWERING of Reformation music took place as a result of the Calvinist movement. Many leaders of this school denounced anthems and choirs, and some even excluded instrumental music and congregational singing. Though Calvin and most of the others never went this far, they did, for the most part, confine themselves to the Psalms; and this very restriction added an austere simplicity which gave eloquent tongue to deep popular emotion. The Psalms were set to a limited number of tunes and sung in unison, to very slow time. New translations were made into French, Dutch, and English, in metrical verse; and tunes were composed for this solemn type of singing. The greatest of the Psalm tune composers was Louis Bourgeois (1510–1561?) of Paris and Geneva, whose *Old Hundredth Doxology* is still sung every Sunday in most Protestant churches. English and Scottish composers carried on his work and produced many excellent tunes. Lacking hymnals, the words were often read out a line at a time ("lined out") by a deacon or precentor, and then sung by the worshipers to one of the half dozen or so tunes that each congregation knew. Such was the music of colonial days in New England.

During much of the time of the early Reformation, the Church of England was undecided as to whether to permit the use of congregational hymns or not. Although admiration for Luther was strong in some quarters, Calvin and the Puritans had even greater influence; and for long it was the Psalms rather than hymns which were sung by the Anglicans. Sternhold and Hopkins, and later Tate and Brady, were the chief translators of Psalms into English verse, the music being largely that of the Geneva and Scottish Presbyterians. A few non-Psalm hymns crept in to the later editions and others were also published. It was not until the days of Isaac Watts (1674–1748), an Independent, that hymn singing made much of an inroad on the Psalms, either in the Church of England or in the various nonconformist chapels. Watts' first book appeared in 1707 and may be called the pioneer modern English hymnbook. It had a reviving effect on the waning Independent, or Congregational, churches, and was also widely used by the Anglicans. For music the old Psalm tunes were still largely employed.

John Wesley (1703–1791) was the next great influence on church music. He not only gave birth to the Methodist movement and rebirth to the whole of Protestantism but in the process he saw the tremendous importance of the singing of hymns. He introduced the practice to many churches which had hitherto been restricting themselves to the Psalms. John Wesley himself published a hymnbook in America, the first hymnbook to be published here. It was his brother Charles who did the largest part of the hymn writing. Indeed Charles became one of the most popular hymn writers of all ages; churches clear round the world have fairly echoed with his stirring words. The music selected to accompany them, culled from many sources, was more lively than ever before. From then on new and expanding editions of hymnals rushed from the presses. Poetry and music were often quite bad but there is no denying that piety was stimulated; and these books had a real influence on Christian theology and feeling. Even the Anglicans now forgot their hesitation and began rapidly to introduce hymns, though retaining the Psalms also in chanted form. The Czecho-German Moravians and the Welch Methodists also became prolific hymn producers. Their tunes were of a higher musical order than those of the English and American composers. In the nineteenth century the Oxford Movement in the Anglican Church not only produced some stirring hymns but sought to restore liturgical emphasis and sung services. But the music used was not in the ancient modes of the Gregorians so much as in the new Romantic styles.

Thus released by the Reformation to introduce new forms of worship, by the Romantic Movement to express itself in uncontrolled emotionalism, and by the Methodist Revival to give vent to the religious thoughts and feelings of the "man in the street," church music now entered upon a new era. Though more popular than it had ever been before, it nevertheless sank imperceptibly but surely into a period of aesthetic decline. Up to the eighteenth century, all the music we have noted had been vigorous, creative, simple, and dignified. Even in the age of the Reformation, when unrestrained outbursts might have been expected, the music was stately and decorous. This did not change all at once. Beethoven (1770–1827), at the beginning of the Romantic period, and even César Franck (1822–1890) toward the end, carried on much of their work in the classic tradition; and so also did many of the lesser men. Samuel Sebastian Wesley, a grandnephew of John's, though an Anglican, rarely allowed himself to fall below chaste composition. There is much from Beethoven, Franck, and Mendelssohn; some from Mozart, Schumann, and Schubert, and even a little from Wagner—which is

worthy of being used by the Church. None of these men, with
the possible exception of Beethoven and Franck, can be placed
alongside of Handel, Bach, Gibbons, Byrd, Luther, Palestrina,
or the Gregorians, as those who can lift men to God on the wings
of pure worship.

Of the Victorian hymns what shall we say? Many of them we
recognize as almost great, and a few even as great. Others have
a "something" about them at which none but a cold critic dare
turn up his nose. Music which for several generations has held
the love and loyalty of millions upon millions of serious-minded
people cannot be dismissed with a shrug. *The King of Love My
Shepherd Is* and *Holy, Holy, Holy* by Dykes; *When Morning
Gilds the Skies* by Barnby; *O Little Town of Bethlehem* by Red-
ner; and others, including some by Sullivan, Stainer, Mason,
Smart, and Monk, are expressive of noble Christian thought and
feeling. On the whole, it is to be feared that catchy, marching, or
mincing rhythm, seductive harmonies and tenor parts, with grace
notes and sliding chromatic half steps, have been granted precedence over dignity and simplicity. Sentiment and delicacy have
displaced power. Strength has given way before loveliness. Today we are discovering with a touch of sadness that the Victorians
were not great enough to express all that Christians ought to be
continuously expressing. Their day is already beginning to draw
toward dusk. The words of many of their hymns deserve and are
beginning to find stronger and more lasting music.

Of the Moody and Sankey type of song we need not say much,
for they never did have high pretentions nor seek to replace the
better type of music in churches. They were composed in particular for evangelistic and prayer services; and not many of
them are to be found in our well-known hymnals for church use.

Anthems of the Victorian age, with certain exceptions, are on
the same plane as the hymns. Pretentious and often artificial
effects mar a great number of them. Soprano trills, close harmony,
bass thunderings, interpolated solo and duet parts, tender inter-
ludes, wordy repetitions, and mighty climaxes are frequent char-
acteristics. Stainer, Speaks, and their school are therefore now
finding themselves to be travelers with Sullivan and Dykes on
the dusky road toward retirement. Those of our grandparents
who had really deep religious feelings to express and knew no

musical manner of expressing them except through the Romantics are, in a way, to be pitied. Some never once had an opportunity to sing to the glories of Bach or Palestrina.

The Moderns

MODERN CHURCH MUSIC is unsettled. For the most part, being educated to no other, Protestant churches are still using Victorian hymns and anthems, even when they stay clear of the "Gospel" type. People enjoy the Victorian songs because they are easily singable, familiar, and associated with their childhood. Choirs and choirmasters like them because they give them such an easy chance to please. But here and there even small churches are seeking something better. When an organist and his pastor are in agreement, the people can usually be brought around.

There are three chief observations to be made about modern church music. First, it is inquisitive and daring. There is a distinct desire to learn more about the values of both new and old forms. Plain song, Catholic and Anglican Renaissance music, German chorales, Calvinistic Psalm tunes, medieval folk songs and carols, Negro spirituals, even Chinese, Indian and African temple music, are all being searched for their religious and artistic values and are being used more and more in many churches in many lands. Note the number of Bach hymns, for instance, in the books of the last few years, as compared with those of fifty years ago. And since hymnbooks are no larger than they used to be, it is obvious that it is the once popular Victorian hymns that are being gradually dropped out, only the better of them managing to survive.

Second, modern music is eclectic and inclusive. This is even more true in England than it is in the United States. The present is the first age in the history of the Church when people have been privileged to sing hymns and anthems from all of the other periods. Up to recently, worshipers have been fairly well limited to those of their own age and denomination. And even now, of course, the bulk of our tunes are still of the Romantic Movement. But nevertheless almost any good hymnal now includes at least some hymns of all types.

Third, there is much fine and distinctive new music being written for the Church in the modern style, both vocal and instrumental. Of course we must admit that the greatest composers of our times—such as Ravel, Rimsky-Korsakov, Stravinsky, Gershwin, and Shostakovitch—have not written primarily for the church. Some of them, however, have had their compositions used in churches, perhaps to their own surprise. There are still others, almost as great—such as Vaughan Williams, Gustav Holst, Clarence Dickinson, David McK. Williams, T. Tertius Noble, Martin Shaw, Olivier Messiaen and the French school— who with true religious insight have set themselves the task of expressing the modern Christian spirit through music. And these have produced much of which our age need not be at all ashamed. Indeed some critics are now saying that the Church is composing at present the best music which it has written since the age of Bach.

Music in Your Church

WE HAVE MADE a rather full analysis of the historical aspects of music as a necessary background for our inquiries into the type of music which we ought to employ today and how it should be handled. As we do this we must keep constantly in mind the spiritual purpose of all church art.

Physical arrangements are important. The choir seats should be disposed in such a way that it is perfectly plain that the choir is leading the congregation in worship and not singing concerts. This is another reason why it seems best for choristers to flank the table and face toward it in line with the axis of the building. In this position they tacitly announce that they stand *with* the congregation in their worship *toward* God, and yet as helpers and leaders. The organ pipes, too, though it is not necessary for them to be hidden, should be divided or placed upon one side, so that none of them are in the middle of the sanctuary or behind the table and cross. The choristers ought, if possible, to be vested, thus not only covering their diversified tastes in clothing but also signifying that they are religious leaders. For they are, in truth, ministers of worship. They should normally enter and depart with the clergy, in procession. The procession need not be down the center aisle unless the church arrangements require it that way. Rhythmic marching is a powerful emotional stimulant and can be used as such in the Church as well as in the army. We need hardly be reminded, however, that a choir is not a military organization, and that it should never show itself off, whether through sound, appearance, or action. Like the minister, the choir should keep itself as inconspicuous as possible except when its turn comes to take a leading part. It is important that the organist be invisible to the congregation at all times, for his motions are bound to be distracting.

Quartets, duets, and solos are happily being used less and less frequently in our churches. The reasons for this are sound. For one thing, it is more difficult for a choirmaster to control a soloist or even a quartet than a chorus. Such singers generally wish to choose their own selections and yet are often incapable of doing so. For another thing, soloists, or members of very small groups, can rarely be anything else than individuals. Their voices are open to frequent criticism on the part of the congregation. Congregations should not attempt to be critics; this ruins worship. Yet it is difficult to maintain the spirit of exalted worship under some church quartets and soloists. If it is necessary to have solo parts in chorus work, the soloist should be warned not to step out from his group or to face even slightly toward the congregation as he sings. This would indicate too much self-consciousness and would be likely to undo whatever worshipful feeling the chorus as a whole may already have created and maintained. The duty of a choir is never to impress the people with its musical skill but to lead them to express themselves, both inwardly and outwardly, toward God. The first requirement in a choir singer, therefore, whether he be paid or not, is that he be an earnest Christian.

Hymns, anthems, and organ voluntaries are at present the chief musical "numbers" in most services. Little by little, however, we should seek to accustom the people to joining in introits, responses, chants, and amens, even though this means reducing the length and number of anthems. Many will not like this at first; but once they sense that it is they themselves, and not the minister and choir only, who are acting in worship, they will be eager to join audibly in the service. The minister or choirmaster has to discipline himself by hard study in the choice of hymns, in order to assist the people in the best possible way to express their various moods. Selecting the right hymn for the right moment is a very difficult art, but a responsive congregation will more than repay the minister for his successes.

As to the type of hymn and anthem to be chosen, it would seem obvious that the strongest and deepest, the most dignified and well written that the people of any given congregation will accept, should regularly be used. At first the members may say that Barnby and Stainer and Sullivan can express their feelings better than Bach and Holst. They will protest that they are but simple folk, accustomed to simple ways, and that only by using tunes that they have known since childhood can they let themselves go and sing. The minister should respect a congregation's viewpoint and be sympathetic and patient. Education, open-mindedness, and practice can often produce miracles. Once a congregation discovers the emotional and intellectual release of really great music, it can usually be counted upon to lose all desire to return to the dulcet sweetness of the Romanticists.

As to simplicity, we must recognize the fact that people are right when they say that hymns for congregational use should be simple. They should be within the range of the average voice, strong and diatonic in their melody, free in rhythm, and for the most part arranged for unison singing. It may be a pleasant surprise, too, for people to discover how simple and singable is much of Bach and the other great ones. Familiarity, however, though obviously desirable, is not a valid touchstone by which to judge a hymn. New hymns can be learned, and when learned are no longer unfamiliar. Many of our ancestors were content with but six or eight tunes. Now we know that even a thousand are not too many for the average mind to retain in memory. Let us not be lazy in our worship!

It is difficult to say what "religious" music is. Many of the chorales of Luther and Bach, many of the Psalms of the Genevans and Scots, were secular songs before being taken over by the Church. Solemn hymns, if given a little rhythmic twist, may sometimes find themselves being played by dance bands. For us it is only necessary to repeat the same test that we make for architecture, painting, drama, dancing or anything else: art is Christian when it expresses Christian feelings or Christian thoughts. We are not saying that Bach is more Christian than Dykes, or plain song than Lowell Mason. What we are saying is that, after just a small amount of training, most people will find that the compositions of the masters will give them more satisfactory and more nearly complete release for their Christian and worshipful impulses than will weak, vapid, unskilled, or thoughtless compositions. First there must be a sincere desire really to worship. Then worship will seek for adequate modes of expression. Great thoughts and great feelings search inexorably for great forms.

CHAPTER VI

Church Literature

~~~~~~

IN THIS CHAPTER, as in most of the others, it is church art rather than Christian art in general with which we are mainly concerned. It is hoped and recommended, however, that the reader will carry on his own pursuit of the wider subject of Christian literature as a whole.

The Bible

CHRISTIANS ARE FORTUNATE in their literary heritage for the Bible is as fine a piece of writing as we have in English. Indeed the translators appointed to the task by King James I did their work so well that the New Testament ranks higher, as literature, in English than it does in Greek. It is in itself a creative artistic production; it is more than an ordinary translation.

Fortunately the English tongue was at its richest at the time when this work was done. English, as languages go, is not old. It is fundamentally Germanic, having been taken over to Celtic Britain by the Angles and Saxons, and other German and Danish nations which invaded the island soon after the Roman withdrawal. Each of the invading tribes had its own tongue, but all sprang from the same root. Gradually, in England, the languages fused and formed what is now known as Anglo-Saxon, or Old English. To this were added certain elements, both from the Celtic and also from the Latin which Caesar's legions had left behind them. Before the process was complete, the Normans came (1066); though also Germanic in origin, they had absorbed French ways and French speech during several generations of living in France.

In England, this Frenchified language of the Normans was now mated with the as yet not quite mature Anglo-Saxon, and English was the result of the union. Its roots were largely Germanic but the French-Latin strain brought by the Normans made it far richer, more flexible, courtly, and sophisticated than it could otherwise have been. The new language did not wax strong immediately. Chaucer and Wyclif, writing about three hundred years after the invasion, were still much more Anglo-Saxon than were the King James's translators, or Shakespeare, or Cranmer. Little by little the guttural harshness and many of the unnecessary and irregular endings began to wear off. By the time that "the most high and mighty King James" was able to order the translation of the Bible into English, English had reached a very high point of literary beauty.

Soon after Shakespeare and King James, a decline began in the simple beauty of this new and vigorous English tongue because of the rapid introduction of terms taken largely from the Greek and the Latin. Many of these classical words were long and cumbersome; the peculiar charm of the Marian, Elizabethan, and Jacobean English forever disappeared. It was fortunate that Cranmer, Spenser, and Shakespeare, as well as Tyndale, Coverdale and the King James translators lived at a time of marvellously vigorous and beautiful English.

There had been translations of the Bible before King James. The Venerable Bede, in the eighth century, had undertaken to translate the Gospel of John into Anglo-Saxon; a hundred years later King Alfred and others had rendered the Psalms and certain other portions. Then after a lapse of four hundred years, John Wyclif and his helpers translated the whole of the Bible from the Latin into Middle English. Another century passed, and William Tyndale, stirred by the work of Luther and by the great editor of the Greek New Testament, Erasmus, again took up the labor. Living as an exile in Germany and under fearful danger, he managed to finish the New Testament and part of the Old before he was arrested and put to death in 1536. Miles Coverdale, using as his basis all of Tyndale that was finished, and working under the protection of Henry VIII, carried on the task.

The greatest work of all was that of a committee of fifty scholars appointed by King James I, who worked from 1604 to

1611. These translators drew upon all predecessors, and thus it may be truly said that their version is not the work of just a few individuals but rather of a whole period in English history. No translation could have been made under more favorable auspices; and though modern renderings are often more accurate, none can vie with King James's for sublimity of diction and poetic and spiritual insight. In the words of the Preface of the translators, the Bible is an "inestimable treasure, which excelleth all the riches of the earth; because the fruit thereof extendeth itself, not only to the time spent in this transitory world, but directeth and disposeth men unto that eternal happiness which is above in heaven." It contains legend and story, history and lore, poetry and philosophy, sermons and devotional reading, description and essays, science and travel tales, Gospels, epistles, and visions. Age after age it has instructed children, strengthened the middle-aged, and comforted the old. It has been translated into over a thousand tongues and is the most often printed and most constantly read book, by far, which the world has produced. Many have read it again and again from cover to cover. Few people of any land or language, if they can read at all, have not perused at least some portions of this priceless work. Its influence, not only upon literature but also upon art, education, law, morality, social customs, science, government, philosophy, and religion, has been incalculable. The Bible has been woven into the very stuff of our civilization.

It is a mistake to consider the Bible as one book, for it is a collection of many. Nor does it maintain one uniform level either of literary value or of morality and religious insight. The Old Testament is a record of the growth and development, both religiously and in all other ways, of the Hebrew nation. To the Hebrews we are eternally indebted for having gone deeper into the search for an adequate experience of God, both as a group and as individuals, than has any other civilization. In Hebrew history there were some people who knew more of the heart of God and lived more closely in his presence than others. Not all of these people wrote down their insights. Sometimes, no doubt, those who understood less wrote more. Hence the broad and many-sided humanity of the Bible—there is no priggishness in it. Yet all the way through, whatever the subject of the writer, there stands unclouded and clear the same sure mountain of faith in Jehovah.

Certain difficulties arise for us moderns in understanding this ancient set of writings, so far removed from the scientific outlook and social experiences of today. One difficulty is caused by the fact that the books are not arranged in the chronological order of their writing; this makes it hard for us to note their ideological developments. Another is that even within some of the individual books (for example, Genesis or Isaiah) there is a mixture of authorship, thus causing confusion as to dates and allusions. Another difficulty resides in the fact that many people have been taught that the Bible is so holy that the authors cannot possibly have made any mistake whatsoever, whether in history, science, or morality. We are asked by these people to believe as God's truth many old legends as to the origin of the world; God's exclusive care for, and frequent intervention on behalf of, a repeatedly sinning nation; the superhuman acts of certain heroes; and many sub-Christian statements of moral standards.

Miracle stories also, though they often have profound truth in them, cannot be easily credited today on a factual level. The Hebrews undoubtedly believed, for instance, that the world, the heavens, and all that in them is, were made in six days, God resting upon the seventh. We need not believe it just because the Hebrews did. We have data that they did not have. To us, the significant aspect of that story is not its scientific statements but the magnificent faith of the Hebrews that, back of all creation, conceiving all, nurturing all, guiding all, brooding over all, was God. Whatever the scientific postulations of Genesis may be, the spiritual truth is superb, glorious, and faithful. That is what we must never forget! And also, purely from the viewpoint of literature, we may revel in the exceeding beauty of the poem of creation as it is contained in the first chapter of Genesis.

The Church on the whole has realized that not all of the Bible is of equal value. Selections have been made to be read in churches, and certain passages have been singled out for frequent reading because of their especial beauty, truth, and practical helpfulness, or their narration of the lives of Jesus and St. Paul. Such a selection as this is called a "lectionary."

In America, at the present time, it is assumed that all Christians own their own Bibles and read them outside of the church. Most probably do. Yet of all the Christians of history in all the lands of the world, including even those living today, a surprisingly small proportion of them have been able to read. For the most part, that which people have learned of the Bible has come through their hearing of it in church, not their reading of it at home. When we stop to consider the fact that, in both the east and west of Europe, through much of Christian history, the Bible has been read in a tongue foreign to its hearers, we are appalled to note how few Christians have had the priceless asset that we Protestant Americans accept as a natural right: reading, and hearing, and understanding for ourselves its precious beauty! We are, from this viewpoint, surely the most privileged Christians in history.

In most so-called "liturgical" churches two extended passages of the Bible are read at every service. One selection consists of a portion of the Old Testament, or of an Epistle of the New Testament, or of some passage from any part of the Bible other than a Gospel. The other selection is from a Gospel. Most Protestants—having been taught that since the Bible is all God's Word it is just as good in one place as another—have for this reason reduced these two readings to one, which may come from any section of the Scriptures. Many times, therefore, in Protestant churches, the Gospel is not read at all. This is a serious omission.

In liturgical churches the Epistle, or other non-Gospel passage, is read from the "Epistle Side" of the sanctuary, that is, the right side when one faces the altar. This is sometimes called the "South Side" since churches were originally "oriented," or headed toward the east. The Gospel is read from the "Gospel Side" or "North Side." In most Roman Catholic churches the book is held by an acolyte, there being no lectern, as the celebrant, facing the altar, chants the reading. At present, however, at least in our country, the Gospel is usually repeated in the local language, from the pulpit, before the sermon.

In addition to these extended readings, frequent brief quotations of the words of the Scripture occur in other parts of both Roman Catholic and Protestant services. The introit (or introductory dialogue of minister and people or choir); the call to worship; the antiphons or responsive readings (generally of

Psalms, often ordered in such a way that the whole Psalm Book is read through frequently); most of the anthems; many of the hymns and prayers; special readings for communion services and other sacraments; the ascriptions and benedictions; and certain other materials in the service are from the Bible. In some churches there are also Biblical songs or canticles, which are chanted: such as, the *Magnificat* ("My soul doth magnify the Lord"); the *Nunc Dimittis* ("Lord, now lettest thou thy servant depart in peace"); the *Venite* ("O come let us sing unto the Lord"); and the *Jubilate Deo* ("O be joyful in the Lord"). Thus is the Bible woven in and out of the whole ritual, affording the service not only a solid foundation in God's verbal revelation of himself but also a literary charm which makes a well-conducted Christian service a thing of exceeding beauty.

The public reading of the Bible in an intelligible way, with dignity, clarity, and sense, is not easy. The average minister might very profitably spend more time in preparation for his reading than he generally does. The art of elocution is a church art not to be neglected.

Prayers and Prayer Books

NEXT AFTER THE BIBLE in literary importance are the prayers. Here again we are highly fortunate in our English heritage. For the Book of Common Prayer came out of the same general age in history as did Shakespeare and the King James Bible and possesses the same quiet, unaffected, reverent beauty that these other books do. The Psalms and certain other Bible passages quoted in the Book of Common Prayer are from the translations by Miles Coverdale, antedating the King James version by about seventy-five years. Thus there are many differences of wording, the most common being the use of "trespasses" instead of "debts" in the Lord's Prayer. In this case the rendering of Coverdale is more accurate but in most cases the King James is better. The man who did most of the work on the Prayer Book was Archbishop Thomas Cranmer, who paid for his Protestantism with his life, under Queen Mary in 1556. Cranmer was one of the great literary geniuses of our language. His translations, adaptations, and original compositions are all in the highest of taste and imbued with depth and devotion of spirit.

A Prayer Book should be in the possession of every Christian whether he belongs to the Episcopal Church or not. Some say that publicly conducted prayers should issue spontaneously from the heart of the leader rather than being read, and surely this right of freedom ought to be maintained and used, as it was in the ancient Church. Most people who are charged with the duty of leading others in prayer soon find that, without some literary aid, they fall into their own habitual phraseology Sunday after Sunday and become even more stereotyped and less spontaneous than the Prayer Book itself. And though many faults can be found in this book, even by Episcopalians, and though there are many other prayer books and worship guides, and many good and usable prayers both new and old which are not included in the Prayer Book, nevertheless any leader of worship will do very wisely if he reverts frequently to this book. For both in religious insight and fervor and in literary style there is not now nor is there ever likely to be in our language another work its equal.

Prayers are of a number of sorts, and a worshiper ought to be able to tell them apart and recognize their forms and uses. There are adorations, thanksgivings, confessions, petitions, intercessions, and dedications. If possible these should be kept separate, so that each prayer in a service is a unity and thus easier for a group to follow. Certain famous and often used prayers are so beautiful, so helpful, and so well known that they ought to be learned by heart by every Christian child. Among these are the Lord's Prayer; the General Confession ("Almighty and most merciful Father"); the General Thanksgiving ("Almighty God, Father of all mercies"); the Collect for Peace ("O God, who art the Author of peace and Lover of concord"); and the prayer of St. Chrysostom, taken from the Greek Liturgy ("Almighty God, who hast given us grace").

Differing forms of prayers should also be understood. A litany, for instance, is a responsive prayer, a dialogue before God, between leader and people. An invocation is a calling upon God for his presence and blessing. A bidding prayer is one in which the leader suggests subjects and the congregation prays in silence after each subject. A suffrage is a short intercessory prayer with responses in the nature of a litany.

The most interesting of all the various prayer forms is the collect. This is a brief prayer, simple in spirit and wording, binding up into one sentence a single significant thought. A true collect is in five parts: the address to God; an attributing phrase about God (generally introduced by the words "who art," "who dost," "who canst" or the like); a petition or intercession in terms of that attribute; an explanation of the purpose of the prayer (generally using the words "that so," "so that," "that," "so we may" or the like); and the closing statement, "through Jesus Christ our Lord." Go through the Sunday collects in the Prayer Book some day and see how one after another of them falls into this pattern. Here, for instance, is one priceless example:

O God, who hast prepared for those who love thee such good things as pass man's understanding; Pour into our hearts such love toward thee, that we, loving thee above all things, may obtain thy promises, which exceed all that we can desire; through Jesus Christ our Lord. *Amen.* (Collect for the 6th Sunday after Trinity)

Another aspect of the Prayer Book with which all should be familiar is the various responses and versicles. For, though they are not universally employed, they are often heard in churches of many different denominations; and surely a worshiper ought, in whatever service he happens to find himself, to be equipped to enter co-operatively into the service. Indeed if such practices were generally learned, the visiting of Christians from one denomination to another would be more common, and ecumenical Christianity immeasurably furthered. When the minister begins, "O Lord, open thou our lips," the people should immediately reply, "And our mouth shall show forth thy praise." When he says, "Praise ye the Lord," the people respond, "The Lord's name be praised." Prayers are often introduced by the phrase, addressed to the people, "The Lord be with you," to which the proper response is, "And with thy spirit." Then there are the *Kyrie Eleison* (which is Greek for "Lord, have mercy"); and the *Sursum Corda* (Latin for "Lift up your hearts!"); the *Sanctus* ("Holy! holy! holy!"); the *Agnus Dei* ("O Lamb of God!") and the like, all of which have their proper responses. The "Amen" after a prayer means in Hebrew, "So let it be"; and is correctly used as a congregational or choir response to a pastoral prayer. Though we all know this we use it too seldom.

The more that a congregation can thus put itself audibly into the prayers, the easier does it become for them to attain true worship. We should constantly remember that the minister does not worship *for* us but *with* us. No Christian, therefore, should fail to become acquainted with these historic dialogues and ejaculations of praise and prayer. They are far older than the Episcopal Prayer Book; appear in all the various forms of the Roman Mass and Eastern Liturgies; and some of them can be traced back even to Biblical days.

Signs and Symbols

WHILE WE ARE on this subject of foreign words and phrases, there are two or three literary symbols that might also be explained at this time, for they are often seen displayed in churches, or on liturgical books or bookmarks. One of them is the A and Ω, sometimes combined into a monogram. They are the first and last letters of the Greek alphabet, Alpha and Omega, and refer to God as being the beginning and the end of all things. Another is I H S, also generally seen in monogram form, which, in Greek, are the first two and the last letters of the word "Jesus." A third is I N R I, which is the Latin abbreviation of *Iesus Nazarenus Rex Iudaeorum*, Jesus of Nazareth King of the Jews, the inscription on the cross of our Lord. (John 19:19.) A fourth is the monogram ☧ (X and P, "Chi" and "Rho"), the first two letters of Christ in Greek.

Psalms, Hymns, and Spiritual Songs

THE NEXT MOST IMPORTANT literary form found in churches is the Psalms. These are used by services of all denominations, sometimes spoken responsively, sometimes chanted or sung. In the early Swiss, Scottish, and English Reformation churches, and among early American Presbyterians, Episcopalians, Congregationalists, and Baptists, Psalms were the only songs sung. Many free metrical translations were made, though the average congregation did not have books and knew only a few by heart. Some of the Psalms are still sung by us all; namely, "The King of love my Shepherd is," "O God our help in ages past," and others. In the Reformed churches of the Continent which followed Zwingli rather than Calvin, all music, including the singing of Psalms, was forbidden for some years. In a few other denominations, too, this rule was followed. Such austerity could not be maintained for very long.

Hymns, too, are a most important and almost universal literary form of worship. The singing of hymns is a very old usage, having been engaged upon in apostolic times. Today many hymns are based on Biblical texts; others are prayers and should be sung as such. There are hymns of praise and adoration, of confession, petition, intercession, and dedication—all prayers. There are also hymns of edification and exhortation. There are hymns of joy in God, Jesus, the Holy Spirit; hymns of aspiration for all kinds of spiritual qualities; hymns of hope for a better world; hymns specific to certain seasons or services of the Church, such as Christmas, Easter, sacraments, ordination; hymns for the home or personal events, such as childhood, marriage, funeral, memorial; hymns for the civil year and special occasions; and hymns of many other kinds. When a hymn is announced at a service, the worshipers should glance through its words while the preliminary verse is being played by the organist and seek to put themselves into its spirit and specific purpose. Although properly speaking the "Amen" is a response by someone other than the speaker or singer and therefore should not be sung after a congregational hymn, the word has become so associated with the closing of a prayer that it is a good custom to finish prayer hymns, at least, with the "Amen." Such differentiation would require attention on the part of the organist and congregation—which after all is a good thing.

The hymns of the Church are of differing literary standards. Some are glorious in their beauty; others quite shoddy and unworthy. What is it, as far as words are concerned, which makes a good hymn? It is hard to give a brief answer. One must have a wide literary background as well as a deep religious experience in order to be able to judge a hymn fairly. Let us state a few general principles.

A good hymn should first of all be an agent for the gathering which uses it to express some phase of its religious experience before God. A hymn intended to be sung by a group should therefore never use the word "I," but always "we." This is so obvious a rule that one is surprised to see how often it has been broken. A hymn, like a prayer, should generally be objective; that is, it should turn the thoughts of the user away from self and toward God. Introspective hymns are sometimes called for; confession and aspiration are necessary for the Christian group as well as for individuals. Introspection, however, should consume but a brief part in the whole service and can generally be taken care of by prayer or Bible reading; there should therefore never be more than one introspective hymn in any one service, and this should not be long, morbid, or extreme. This is a very important principle. The average service is probably better off without any introspective hymns at all. Such as are used should begin and end in full recognition of God's majesty, love, and goodness.

Again, a hymn should be exalted in style, not stilted or given to literary trickery; should avoid the painfully obvious, the pretty, the sentimental, or the abject. It should always have intellectual as well as emotional content, be dignified, restrained, earnest, uninvolved. If possible each stanza should be a sentence unto itself. At the same time a hymn should not fear to make such use of rich poetic imagery as is calculated to bring men into the presence of God's splendor. And surely it is an axiom that the splendor of God can be apprehended very much more easily through the use of majestic, moving language than through words which are threadbare.

It is unfortunate that when English was at its poetic best—at the time of the writing of the Prayer Book and the translations of the Bible—the poets were not encouraged to write hymns. At that time hymns were not yet approved in the Anglican and Reformed churches, and the great poets of the day—Shakespeare, Spenser— did not care for the more or less hackneyed task of versifying the Psalms. However, some of the best poets of all ages subsequent to this have been eager to lend their talents to the writing of hymns. Also many great poems which were not originally intended to be hymns have, with few changes, been so used. Although too many writers of inadequate poetic skill have written for our hymnals, there are really enough good hymns in our books so that Christians may be proud of their general literary merit.

Many of our hymns which undeniably are of poor literary quality will long continue to be loved. We must respect the conservatism of the average person; admit that not all Christians are well educated in poetics and that the needs of these people must certainly be met; and expect to change group habits but gradually. Nevertheless we ought all to seek to teach ourselves how to separate the adequate hymns from the inadequate, to improve our own standards, and to help our fellow Christians to do the same. For only the greatest words matched with the greatest music can express the greatest thoughts.

The Sermon

THE SERMON IS not a lecture, oration, declamation, recited essay, nor book review. It is a distinctive art form for a distinctive purpose. It should be specifically addressed to the needs of a particular congregation. It should, in these days, be brief, clear, with several easily remembered points, unified around a manageable theme, expressing always a fundamental Christian faith and seeking to establish people therein. It should be based directly upon some passage of the Bible, most often the Gospels. It should be one phase of the whole service, full cousin to the invitation, prayers, hymns, anthems, and ascriptions. Each sermon should be instructive as well as inspiring, being related to some course of progressive and comprehensive thinking, such as the church year. The sermon is a part of what might be called the revelatory aspect of worship, in which God speaks to man, the minister being at the moment, humbly but boldly, the prophet and the teacher come from God. With what care and prayer, then, must the minister prepare himself not only to speak for God but to speak for God well! And with similar care and prayer should the congregation prepare itself to receive his words and to make vigorous creative response.

Personal Reading

CHRISTIAN LITERATURE, as distinct from church literature, includes much of our poetry, fiction, drama, philosophy, sociology, history, and biography.

The field is too enormous for us to examine in detail. Of Christian poets, Dante, Milton, Blake, Donne, Browning, Emerson, Laurence Housman, W. H. Auden, T. S. Eliot, and many others, should be on our list. We should also all own two or three good anthologies of religious poetry. Some of the great Christian novels, such as those by Dostoievsky and Tolstoi, should be read and reread. The dramatists, philosophers, and historians should not be neglected. Biography is full of stimulating stories of Christian saints, heroes, martyrs, and missionaries, some of them in excellent literary form. There are countless other books on the Bible, economics, sociology, psychology, politics, and the peace movement, which can be called Christian expression.

The riches to be discovered in devotional literature are amazing and easily available. None who reads this summary should go to bed tonight without looking on his shelves for his father's old dusty copy of the "Confessions" of St. Augustine. Let him browse around in it for a while and it can almost be guaranteed that he will begin a full reading of it the next morning. Then there are the *Imitation of Christ, The Little Flowers of St. Francis, Pilgrim's Progress,* the works of Meister Eckhart, St. Catherine of Siena, Loyola, St. Francis de Sales, William Law, John Wesley, George Fox, William Penn, John Woolman, Baron von Hügel, Forbes Robinson, Evelyn Underhill, Thomas Kelly, and Harry Emerson Fosdick. These all are on the Christian's "must list." The sooner one becomes acquainted with them, the happier he will be. They will all aid him in deepening his spirit of worship and therefore his ability to worship in church.

CHAPTER VII

Drama and the Dance

~~~~~~

DRAMA IN CHURCH is not a frill superimposed upon religion or worship in order to make it more attractive or to fill up empty seats in a languishing evening service. Christianity is naturally an intense and vivid experience and requires dramatic expression. And the purpose of drama, like that of every art, is to express experience.

Drama is a highly social art. A painter can finish his work and go off and leave it in a shop, gallery, or drawing room, where it may be enjoyed by a succession of individuals, none of whom has any connection with the others. But a play, like a symphony or an anthem, is an act of common creation and common appreciation on the part of many people. Not only do author, actors, directors, producers, designers, costumers, stage setters, make-up men, electricians, architects, and many others, share in every performance, but the audience also takes its part. The more actively the audience participates, the more social is the art. No drama is really complete until either the active or the vicarious participation of the whole assembly is achieved. Indeed it might almost be said that a good play has no audience. The people are all actors, the leaders being just a few drawn out from among the many to represent them all and to give expression to the moods of the group.

Distinction should be made between drama, Christian drama, and church drama. Drama is the expression of human experience or feeling through the organized portrayal, by living persons, of selected phases of life or character. Christian drama is the dramatic expression of *Christian* experience or feeling. Church drama is such an expression in *church* as an act of worship on the part of a Christian fellowship. To have Christian drama it is first of all necessary to have a Christian playwright, Christian actors and other participants, and a Christian congregation. To have church drama these people must be united in common worship in church. Not all Christian drama is for the production in church. Many Christian plays are staged in schools and colleges, in homes, out of doors, or in commercial theaters. The test of a play's Christianity is not where it is produced but whether or not it expresses Christian ideas or feelings. Church drama is definitely an expression of Christian worship in church.

According to this definition, Christian, though not church, drama may sometimes be produced merely for the purpose of giving outlet to clean Christian fun. Acting is not necessarily to be judged as non-Christian just because it is gay. Light comedy or even farce, vaudeville, skits or charades, though they can never be church drama, may at times be Christian drama. Social dancing, tap dancing, musical games, indeed almost all games, are but variants of the dramatic art; and when they give expression to the desire for wholesome Christian mirth they are surely part of Christian life. Even when plays are produced for the sole end of making money for a church they may nevertheless be performing two desirable Christian functions: giving the young a chance to be of service to the Cause; and allowing them an opportunity to kick up their heels in sheer Christian hilarity. Such plays, however, especially when admission fees are charged, ought to be in the parish house, not the body of the church. There are, these days, few churches which would deny their junior members such natural outlets for good Christian recreation. Christian drama may have the further aim of being educational. Bible stories, moral problems, social issues, are brought before both adults and children in dramatic form in order to teach needed lessons or to induce unselfish living. Motion pictures and radio are being used more and more, both in religious and in secular schools or programs, for this end.

As the Gospel story is naturally dramatic its presentation can be very effective Christian education. The danger is that such plays will, under unskilled handling, degenerate into mere propaganda; but the danger can be avoided. When teaching seeks to impress certain ideas or dogmas, or to produce certain effects upon people, it becomes propaganda. When it gives scope to an honest search for truth or for a wider experience, knowledge, or skill, it is an art. Such educational plays, however, though often admittedly artistic and Christian, are not church plays and ought to be acted in the parish house and not in the church.

The Dramatic Element in Church Worship

EVERY CHURCH SERVICE has in it certain dramatic elements. The minister himself, in one of his functions, is an actor, the chief actor of the congregation. In his leadership of the services Sunday by Sunday, through his readings and administration of the sacraments, he aids the people to give dramatic expression to their moods and their faith. His gestures and motions are of great importance. A hand in benediction gives a meaning quite unlike that of a clenched fist. A minister who slouches in his chair or crosses his legs is failing to meet the needs of sensitive worshipers who wish their leader to express in his conduct their own earnestness and devout attention.

So too is the choir a group of actors. Their deportment, posture, marching, no less than their singing and responsive reading, give organized and formal tongue to the feelings of the people. A choir moving with dignity, earnestness, and a determined tread signifies something quite different from that which one coming in with careless demeanor or listless lips betokens. Dignity, grace, bodily and facial control are of great importance. An attitude of inattention or flippancy, during prayer, sermon, or reading, is sure to communicate itself to the people. The choir is at times almost a tableau and must learn how to be motionless, with eyes fixed upon the symbol, the action, or the leading actor of the moment.

And so also, where they exist, the speaking and rhythmic choirs, and likewise the elders or deacons, and ushers, are leaders in the various phases of the liturgical movement of the church service; and insofar as the liturgy is dramatic these people are actors.

The sacraments of the Lord's Supper and of baptism are the two high points of liturgical action in church worship, and hence the most dramatic. In communion, the table stands for the table of our Lord in the Upper Room. The bread and wine represent not only the necessary sustenance of all life as it is supplied by God to men, but also, and chiefly, the body and blood of Jesus Christ. The elders or deacons are the apostles. The minister takes the place, in deep humility and agony of spirit but with a vivid reality, of our Lord himself at the head of the table. "This is my body; this is my blood," are the words of an actor representing Someone other than himself. It is only because we have used the word "actor" erroneously or derogatorily for so long that we object to it in this connection. Priest, minister, celebrant, leader, officiant, are all words which mean, basically, the same thing: namely, doer, performer, actor, one who effects things on behalf of or in leadership of others. In baptism, too, we have a highly dramatic act, particularly so when the candidate is placed completely under the water, but nevertheless plainly dramatic even in the symbolism of a few drops upon his head. Both of these sacraments are stylized and symbolic, but they are nevertheless dramatic in their every motion. So too are the presentation of the weekly offering; the giving of rings at a wedding; and the sending and grouping of flowers, and the public burial of the body, at a funeral.

In addition to these common means of ceremonial expression, there are other exercises of devotional dramatics which are sometimes used in church and might very well be more often used. Plays may occasionally be substituted for the sermon. Or whole services, from prelude to postlude, may be definitely planned as dramatic services, engaged in by minister, organist, singing and speaking choirs, readers, dancers, ushers, and congregation. The most common of such co-operative dramatic activities in our American churches occur at Christmas time. It is quite general on the Sunday evening preceding Christmas for churches to employ organ music, choir anthems, readings, unison and responsive prayers, tableaux, the march of the Magi, congregational carols, the lighting of candles, and the taking forward of "white gifts" to the manger, as varied phases of a unified and touchingly sincere dramatic service.

Similar services could also be used at Advent, Epiphany, Ash Wednesday, Maundy Thursday, Good Friday, Easter, Pentecost, All Saints' Day and individual saints' days, Thanksgiving

Day, Forefathers' Day, and local anniversaries. Just as the Christian experience runs the whole gamut of emotion from deep sorrow and contrition to exalted joy, from birth to death and resurrection, so has the Church provided a suitable season for the natural outlet of each of these moods. Drama opens up every one of these phases of man's emotional being and gives him opportunity to lose himself in the ecstacies of complete spiritual expression. Such dramatic services should not, perhaps, be utilized on all of these occasions every year; but certain of them, beloved because of their beauty or their associations, may be frequently repeated. A good service does not become tarnished with exposure.

A Look at History

NOR IS THIS TYPE of dramatic service new to religious or Christian history. Corporate worship was probably begun by bodily motion and dancing. Evelyn Underhill quotes a story of Osbert Sitwell's about a traveler in an equatorial forest who saw an ape, one night, bowing deeply before a full moon. The traveler testified that he "had seen," in that act, "the birth of religion."[2] Bowing and other such motions of adoration soon advanced into dancing. At first all of the people engaged in it, in some specified place. Then one or more of their number were chosen to come out of the group and lead the others. The chief dancer, or actor, became the priest; and the center of these ritual dances and actions an altar or stage.

Though priests were thus set off from laymen, the people long continued to have a conspicuous share in the actions, songs, and responses. In Greece the chorus of dancers and singers, accompanied by the flute-playing carolers, stood for the city as a whole. In China the emperor himself, at the magnificent Altar of Heaven in Peking, was the chief priest; but he was surrounded by officials, musicians, and dancers whose every word and motion were prescribed in the Book of Rites and meticulously performed. The altar was a mighty stage upon which, in concentric circles, the celebrants—both emperor and laymen—all walked and

[2] "The Golden Sequence," Dutton, p. 161.

engaged upon their duties. Thus, in both of these great centers of civilization, were sacrifice, gesture, acting, singing, dancing, playing, praying, all parts of one service; they centered upon an altar and were engaged in by a large group of worshiping participants and spiritually active spectators.

The Greek tragedies were a part of the religious festivals of the god Dionysius. It was about his altar that the chorus danced. And it was in his honor that the ideals of Greek ethics and religion were set forth through the representation of the lives of ancient gods and heroes. It is of no little significance that our word "tragedy" is derived from τράγος and ἀείδειν, a "goat," and "to sing." Tragedy is the celebration, or representation, of the rôle of the victim of some sacrificial, exalting, or catastrophically significant experience. Before the altar all the elements of life were gathered in a mighty processional—music, dancing, athletics, military exercises, horsemanship, household arts—and were offered to the god in colorful and dramatic fashion. As a climax to the festivities, the great plays of Aeschylus, Sophocles, and others were performed.

Yet, for good or for ill, it was not from these Greek plays that the drama of Western Europe arose. Greek drama sank gradually into vulgar and uninspired comedy, and the Rome of the Empire still further debauched it. Because of the obscenity of the late Roman stage, the Church was compelled to condemn it, thus turning the conscience of Europe for centuries against the theater. But human nature, and no less Christian nature, demanded dramatic expression; and during these centuries the requirement was met in the services of church worship, primarily the Mass. For the Mass, as we have seen, though not a play, does contain marked dramatic elements.

This was not enough to satisfy the need. Out of the soul of men struggling fiercely to be Christian in an evil world grew a whole new dramatic art. Some have thought that the medieval religious plays were born of certain interpolations into the Mass called "tropes." And though these undoubtedly had much influence, their parenthood cannot be unqualifiedly established. The tropes were pertinent Biblical stories inserted into the Mass by individual priests who sought thus to enliven and add interest to it. They were not acted but chanted, a single priest often reading the lines belonging to two or more characters. A whole series of Passion Week, Good Friday, and Easter tropes gradually came into use and attained great popularity with both priests and people. Since they were seen to be attracting interest to themselves at the expense of the central theme of the Mass, church authority transferred them to services other than the Mass. Then it was—in about the tenth century—that some of the tropes became the basis for expansion, rewriting, and finally dramatic representation. Such productions were performed in Latin, chanted (not spoken) by priests, and employed only unrealistic gestures and motions; they served either as independent plays or as parts of certain daily devotions, in church. At first they were not condemned by the higher church powers; but little by little undoubted abuses began to creep into them, and it was finally altogether forbidden to produce them in churches.

In the meanwhile, no doubt under the influence of this nascent church drama, laymen in the guilds had also been experimenting with religious theatricals; when the Church finally rejected its own plays, the laymen were ready to take them up. Thus there was a marriage between the distinctively church drama and the secular but still thoroughly Christian drama of the guilds. The child was the glorious body of thirteenth-century religious—but non-church—plays. These were written in the vernacular languages, and at first were produced on the porches of the churches or in the squares in front. There were "mysteries," which told of the sweep of God's purpose of redemption for man; and there were "miracle plays," about saints or Biblical characters. These plays were arranged in cycles, beginning with the creation of the world, and ending with the final judgment. Each play was enacted by a separate guild. Many of these are left to us, of particular interest being those of York, Townley, Chester, and Coventry in England. "Pageants," which were originally wagons, or floats, transported the various plays of the cycles to different parts, or "stations," of town, where successive audiences awaited their arrival.

Eventually many of these plays also degenerated; jokes were inserted, buffoonery came to crowd out spirituality, and the church leaders were compelled once more to disapprove. "Moralities," whose characters were personified virtues, then became popular, and these persisted down to the days of Ben Jonson and William Shakespeare. Though the background and ideology of the mysteries, miracles, and moralities were Christian, they did not have any function as church liturgy, nor were they acted in churches. In spite of the head-shaking of the Church they did not rapidly disappear and exerted a marked influence on Elizabethan and all subsequent drama.

The Reformation, with its emphasis upon simplicity and puritanism, took a definite stand against dramatic plays in church; so for a number of generations both branches of the Church were left without any means of such dramatic expression. Thus deserted by its most natural exponent, representational acting had no recourse but to fall largely into the hands of the secular theater, where it has for the most part remained ever since. Here one of its chief purposes has been to make money for owners and producers, and here the people have rarely been expected to be anything more than the audience. Fortunately, however, there have been notable and encouraging exceptions to this general commercializing process. A revival of Christian drama, both outside the Church and within, has taken place of recent years, as well as a revival of non-commercial secular drama in the "Little Theater" movement, summer theaters, schools, colleges, and churches.

In Germany, under the stimulation of Gerhardt Hauptmann, Reinhardt Sorge, Rudolph Steiner, Max Reinhardt, and others, especially in the period between the two world wars, the Christian dramatic revival won wide popularity. Groups of wandering players, most of them young, with no thought of making money but only of giving scope to their natural dramatic urge, went from town to town and produced in schools, in universities, and out of doors, their sincere and well-acted plays. Many of these were thoroughly religious. The *Totentanz*, or "Dance of Death," a modernization of the medieval morality *Everyman*, was the most popular subject represented. There were many variations of this theme, but the theme was always the same: the inevitability and the beauty of death. I shall never forget seeing one of these bands of German young people as they produced a thrilling version of the *Totentanz* before a Chinese student group in Peking. Being chiefly a dance, with music but no words, it spoke an international language; and the intensity of the emotion among these Oriental and largely non-Christian observers aroused by this European and thoroughly Christian play was surprising and extraordinary.

In France, too, between the wars, there was a similar movement, begun by the Belgian Maeterlinck and carried on mainly by Paul Claudel. Claudel had also a distinguished career as diplomat both in the Far East and as French ambassador to the United States, but he will live in fame rather as a poet and the author of mystical and Biblical dramas. In England religious plays gained wide popularity during the second war and still retain it. Under the leadership of Elliott Martin Brown and the Religious Drama Society, plays on Christian themes have been presented before large groups in churches, schools, clubs, unions, and soldiers' shelters. Laurence Housman, Dorothy Sayers, and T. S. Eliot are among the leaders in this revival. In the United States Eugene O'Neill has written successful mystical plays; Thornton Wilder has some interesting masques and moralities; and Fred Eastman has done sincere and successful work, not only in chancel pageantry but also in modern plays, of religious and social concern, for the parish house. Among other Englishmen and Americans who have written Christian stage plays are Marc Connelly, Bernard Shaw, Charles Rann Kennedy, Albert Johnson, John Masefield, Geoffrey Whiteworth and Ernest Rhys.

Church Drama Today

IN CONSIDERING OUR problem today we must remind ourselves again of the distinction between Christian plays which are to be performed in the parish house and church plays for production in the church proper as a means of worship. The choice of those for the stage is a wider one than of those for the chancel. Among stage plays suitable for Christian production are a few Greek dramas, especially those of Euripides, which are highly religious and almost Christian in their viewpoint. These should be produced out of doors if possible. A church with large resources and a sophisticated congregation might specialize in Greek drama, as do some colleges, producing one each year in its garden theater. There are also the many modern plays dealing with world peace, missions, and race problems, with church history and biography, and with problems of social or personal morality, such as those we have noted in the last section. Many of these are of close kin to chancel plays but the difference can generally be perceived. Unless the play is distinctly an avenue of worship it should not be produced in the church or chapel, but if it is such an instrumentality, then the chancel is unquestionably the place for it.

Where shall we find worshipful plays which will be suitable for production in ordinary American churches? Sometimes they can be written by the church groups themselves. This is especially true of Sunday schools and Young People's organizations. Pupils should be encouraged to express themselves in this way. Original dramatizations of Bible stories, particularly at Christmas, Easter, and other festivals, are becoming more and more popular. Plot, setting, and even much of the wording are already provided. For people of all ages, but especially for young people and children, such exercises in dramatics, with no thought of instructing or pleasing a public, can be a creative and hallowing experience.

It should be remembered, however, that the writing and production of plays, whether for the chancel or the stage, are difficult arts, and amateurs can hardly be expected to achieve finished results for congregational worship. The sole object of drama, when there is no one but the participating group present, is to give voice to the experience of the actors and producers. When certain individuals are chosen out of a group to be actors on behalf of others, or when the doors are thrown open to the whole church, then the object is to give voice not only to the actors' and producers' experience but also to the experience of the congregation, and the whole matter becomes more difficult. In drama, as in liturgies, as in music or any other art, though amateurs have their part to play, it is the great masters who can open wide avenues out of others' souls where beginners and dabblers must perforce fail.

Though it is a good creative exercise for a group to write its own plays to be produced for its own group only, it is far better, if the play is to be given at a public church service, that the works of the masters be used. The Chicago Theological Seminary will supply any inquirer with a selected list of good religious dramas, including both parish house and chancel plays. Several good books on Biblical dramas are now available. Denominational bookstores can also make suggestions. Every church should attempt to maintain a drama guild as surely as it does a choir. Or, at the very least, it should try to get the interested people together from time to time to express, for the church, the worshipful needs of the church as a whole through drama. The minister should be the adviser and guide to this guild, as he is to the choir; and others appointed must be willing to set themselves seriously to study the problems, to read, think, discuss, and to view others' productions. One of the duties of this group would be to make choice of the plays to be produced. Only the best plays are worth giving. It is to be expected that a suitable royalty should be paid.

Of the few great modern chancel plays to be purchased, outstanding is T. S. Eliot's "Murder in the Cathedral." This has often been produced in theaters but seldom in its natural setting of a church. Pageants, which are rather elaborate enactments of broad themes with many participants, are now very popular; they are often in pantomime, with musical or scriptural accompaniments. Fred Eastman has done conspicuous and excellent work in this field of art. Of recent years, in our country, a new interest has arisen in Passion Plays in the manner of Oberammergau and other such European grand-scale representations. Americans, however, have not been content to perform these only once in ten years; most churches which have put them on at all have done so annually, except as interrupted by war. Some of them are produced in churches, some in specially built arenas, and some out of doors. Christmas dramatizations in church are now quite customary, ranging from simple tableaux to elaborate pageantry. It is an unimaginative church which does not possess at least a small wardrobe of shepherds', angels', and wise men's garments, and some equipment of star, manger, and shepherds' crooks.

Then there is the whole field of medieval plays. We may have to take certain liberties with them and rewrite or edit them to suit a modern church situation. Nor can we confine ourselves to them alone lest we maintain too continuously an attitude of naïveté, romanticism, and unreality. Medieval plays are often expressive of eternal Christian beliefs and longings. It helps that most of them are easily available in cheap form, have no copyright restrictions, are brief, and are cast for small numbers of actors. Such plays have been found equally suitable for large city congregations such as the Fountain Street Baptist Church of Grand Rapids, and for small churches in the country. As an example of the latter, I think of a tiny church in the hills of Connecticut which for a period of years produced a medieval mystery every Easter Sunday evening. The Cornish *Three Maries*, and *Mary Magdeline and the Apostles* were alternated, each being highly effective. A skilled and sympathetic professor from the State University was invited to act the part of Jesus and to assist in the direction. The setting was simple; the plays were short and understood to be only part of the regular service of worship; the minister led the prayers and read Scriptures; the choir sang the dirges to Bach chorale tunes; the congregation joined in the responses and sang the hymns; and a new conclusion was written for the *Three Maries* which led the people quite naturally up to the climactic hymn, *"Jesus Christ Is Risen Today."* Both of these plays are to be found in the Everyman's Library edition of "Everyman." The expense of production was almost nothing.

Phillips E. Osgood and Russell Bowie have sought to regain for modern production the spirit of medieval plays. Their works can be further adapted if desired or new ones may be written by people who know their craft. The more that congregational prayers, responses, hymns, and other participation are included, the better these plays will serve their creative worship purpose. Dancers and speaking choirs can be introduced into many of them with good effect. If the parts be played anonymously, this also will enhance the devotional spirit among both actors and congregation.

Liturgical Dancing

NO ONE NEED be shocked at our occasional references to dancing in church. Dancing is one of the most naturally expressive of all the arts. From the very beginning of history it has been used to give form to religious impulses. African dances, the dances of American Indians and of Australian aborigines, are

almost entirely religious in their purpose. "Let them praise his
name in the dance," said the Psalmist twice (149, 150); and
there are many other references to the dance in the Old Testament. Although the New Testament does not cite dancing as a
religious exercise, we do find it mentioned in early Christian
history; and until the eighth or ninth centuries choirs of boys
danced in churches, sometimes while Psalms were being chanted.
This practice was later forbidden by papal order; but the Cathedral of Seville in Spain was excepted, and to this day boys still
dance before the altar there. The Reformation also would have
no traffic with dancing; and it has not been much used either in
the Western or Eastern churches for many centuries.

There has been a revival of religious dancing recently both
in Europe and in America. On the stage in America this has been
led by Ruth St. Denis, Ted Shawn, and others. Modern Greek
dancing owes much to Isadora Duncan and to Edith Wynne
Matheson. In schools and colleges the movement has gone far,
especially in the women's colleges. There are also a number of
newly established summer camps which provide instruction and
opportunity for expression through the dance. Among churches,
two of which may be mentioned are St. Mark's-in-the-Bouwerie in
New York, under the Reverend Dr. William Norman Guthrie,
and the Church of Christ at Dartmouth College, in Hanover, New
Hampshire, under the Reverend and Mrs. Chester Fisk. Dr. Von
Ogden Vogt in Chicago, and the Reverend Robert Storer of Dor-
chester, Massachusetts, have also used dancing and drama in their
morning services of worship.

Such liturgical dancing is not stiff or formal. Though there is
necessarily co-ordination of movements when more than one dancer is involved, the motions are the genuine expression of the
participants' attitudes and feelings. This is unlike ballet dancing,
where certain steps are rigidly learned for the sake of effect on
an audience. In church dancing the participants seek to bring
into the open the secret longings and feelings both of themselves
and of the congregation. By their movements they show forth
wonder at God's greatness, praise and adoration, penitence,
prayerful desires, and dedication to his service.

Sometimes just a few young women, clothed in white, go
silently and unannounced into the chancel while a hymn is being

sung, and embody through their motions the same mood that the congregation is simultaneously expressing through its singing. Sometimes the exalted mood of a Psalm can be reinforced with rhythm, notably such a Psalm as the one hundred and fiftieth. On other occasions a special place in the service is reserved for a brief dance. Sunday schools are in a particularly favorable position to use this mode of worship, never as a show or demonstration, but only to give the children free, prayerful, and vigorous outlet for their naturally worshipful emotions. A beginning in this direction has already been made in our churches through gowned processions of choirs, often very affecting, and through the march of the ushers bringing forward the offerings of the people. In churches for the deaf, rhythmic movements of the hands and arms by the choir or by an entire congregation, while the words of the hymns are displayed on a stereopticon screen, often take the place of singing. In most churches a lack of understanding of what can be done, prejudice, and a natural conservatism, have so far largely prevented the development of rhythmic choirs to anything like their full possibilities.

Candle Services

SERVICES OF LIGHTS and candles have also, of recent years, been revived. Though Epiphany is the most notable opportunity for the use of fire and lights, Advent, Christmas, Maundy Thursday, and Easter are also appropriate times. In our Protestant churches young people are often admitted to membership on Palm Sunday, the first communion being Maundy Thursday evening. Where this is the case, a highly effective service for Maundy Thursday, based on the ancient Tenebrae, can be utilized. In this service nine lighted candles are placed in the chancel, one directly in front of the cross, the others on side tables. The electric lights are turned off and the minister reads from the Bible the experiences of sadness, chagrin, and suffering which Jesus underwent during Passion week. His weeping over the city, his shock at the desecration of the Temple, the opposition of the people, the betrayal of Judas, the denial of Peter, the failure of disciples to watch one hour, his trial and condemnation and the culminating shame and pain of the crucifixion, are all recited in brief quotations from the Bible. As each passage is given, a gowned young woman extinguishes one of the candle lights, until finally the one before the cross itself is the only light left. In the traditional Tenebrae service, this candle is then placed behind the cross or the altar, where it is left until Easter morning, the congregation going forth in total darkness and sorrow to await the coming of Easter. This is similar to the medieval service of the Burial of the Cross or Host (in the Orthodox Church the icon from the cross) on Good Friday, and its exhumation on Easter morn. In our suggested version of the Tenebrae, the lone candle is left burning and a long pause takes place while the congregation meditates in dark and solemn silence. At the nadir of this period the choir sings Palestrina's motet, *Tenebrae Factae Sunt;* then the minister, after another pause, goes on to tell of how this one light could not be put out but continued to shine unto the resurrection of a new day; and of how once again, even in this church, new young disciples are now emerging, eager to fire their lives by that of Jesus and to set the world aglow. As the minister thus speaks, the new members come forward from the pews where they have been sitting, light their candles by that of Jesus, place them reverently on his table, and return to their seats. Finally the electric lights go on throughout the whole church as symbolic of the triumph of light in the world. Holy Comunion is administered, first to the new members and then to all.

The service is simple but can be profoundly moving and expressive, not only for the catechumens, who are likely never in their lives to forget it, but also for the congregation as a whole. This is recounted here at length as but one example of many candle services which may have dramatic power.

The Future of Church Drama

MOST OF US need more training than we have had in the proper means of dramatic representation. As in the other arts these techniques have to be mastered. Slovenly work will not produce heavenly results; craftsmanship is something to be earnestly striven for. On the other hand the main thing needed is always a will. If the desire is intensely felt and a few fundamental methods learned, we can be sure that competence and a gratifying beauty will follow. An intelligent, enthusiastic, sincere, and personable director; workers who are willing to read, study, experiment, visit modern theaters, and converse with others who have had experience; a devotional spirit; and a fair amount of courage, are the chief ingredients for success.

The fundamental canons for dramatic art are basically the same as they are for all the other arts: simplicity, clarity, unity, balance, rhythm, appropriateness to environment, and—above all —sincerity. A play, like a picture or any other work of art, must depend upon its central meanings rather than upon tricks or externals. It should therefore develop its theme and characterization not through narratives or explanation but through action, posture, facial expression, and dialogue. Its chief purpose is to express that which is within the soul of a group. It should do this as expeditiously as possible and then bow itself out. Many playwrights of the modern school have interpreted expressionism wholly in terms of "I." An author experiences an object, steeps himself in fellowship with it, and then writes down his own reaction to it, using words, actions, character, situation, theme, mood, conflict, suspense, climax, stage setting, lighting, and the other dramatic elements. We in the Church, however, must never forget that our art is a social one; we are expressing not the "I" but the "we." We are addressing ourselves not to the world in general but to God. A Christian liturgical play is not the expression of an author and his assistants to a church congregation, but the expression of author, assistants, and congregation, in holy partnership, to God.

We should be willing to use the new methods whether physical, verbal or psychological in church drama. As a matter of fact there is a surprising affinity between present-day expressionist drama and the methods and setting of church worship. A church building lends itself favorably to many of the effects that a modern playwright seeks to induce. It does not depend upon painted scenery, realistic stage property, make-up, scene shifting and curtains. It does not seek to separate itself from the people by means of footlights or an orchestra pit. Spotlighting can be used as successfully in church as in a modern theater to denote changes of time and scene. Indeed, a typical church chancel already possesses a balance of cubes and rectangles; a succession of steps leading from the floor to higher levels; height, depth, and dignity; natural shadows and a responsiveness to well-placed and well-manipulated lights; and a sense of familiarity to the congregation. These are some of the exact qualities that many a modern stage designer is at pains to simulate on the less favorably planned theatrical stage.

In the use of simple, poetical speeches, spread among symbolic motions or even dancing, some modern theater plays are startlingly similar to liturgical actions in church. Foreshortening and selection, compressing into a few sentences the presentation of whole-sized characters; or elongation and repetition, enabling certain events or time intervals to be stretched out unnaturally for the sake of emphasizing the significant: both devices are well known not only to the dramatist but to the leader of worship. Costuming by means of gowns with symbolic meaning rather than efforts at realism are also common to both. So also are symbolic stage properties. A lacquer casket is quite enough to indicate the Wise Man's myrrh. A rough wooden box half filled with straw and with a strong light issuing from it represents a manger; a rectangular frame covered with gauze is sufficient for a tomb. A cross, a crown, an altar, an angel, speak directly and simply to those who know what they mean. Elaboration is not needed. Music, the dialogues of litany, congregational prayers with choir amens, or pastoral prayers with congregational amens, hymns, responses, and processions bring the worshipers, in imagination, right up to the altar, table, manger, tomb, or throne; and the more a congregation enters into the action as well as the spirit of a play, the more expressive does the play become for the whole worshiping church.

When the church finally awakes to its opportunity thus to express itself through drama, it will be taking a long step toward becoming once again a group of people who worship God from the depth of their souls. For adequate means of expression help not only to bring forth that which is already there but to develop it. The Church has a natural advantage over the theater in supplying such a means of expression, in that the group present in every service is one which is already prepared for what it is to do and already united. These people know in advance not only the general subject of all possible plays that they may see, but also many of the very words and much of the music to be used. They are eager to throw themselves wholeheartedly into the effort and they earnestly believe that the worship in which they are engaging is the most important single function of their lives.

At no time in its history has the worship of the Church realized all its dramatic possibilities as a conveyor of thought and emotion. Just as church drama was beginning to establish itself in the Middle Ages disruptive forces assailed it. The Church has not yet made up the lost ground, and now that it is beginning to desire to do so, it finds that the secular theater has become entrenched in the popular mind as the chief agent of drama. The task is therefore difficult; the Church cannot expect to accomplish it all in this generation. Ours must still be an age of overcoming prejudice, of pioneering, and of experimentation. The rewards and possibilities for Christian worship along this line are so appealing that it seems to be the duty of every church now, insofar as it can do so, to enter this newly re-opening way of releasing its action-hungry soul.

The drama, combining as it does so many arts (acting, music, literature, speaking, reading, dancing, designing, costuming, painting, lighting, architecture, and many others) is in reality a synthesis of almost all arts. If this art is ever developed to its full possibilities in Church, it can hardly fail to become one of the most telling means of bringing to fulfillment the Church's age-long hope of uniting whole communities in the heartfelt worship of almighty God.

CHAPTER VIII

Painting and Sculpture

PAINTINGS AND SCULPTURE have never been used much in Protestant churches. There have been two reasons for this. One was the feeling, strong at the inception of the Reformation but naturally becoming weaker as time went on, that everything that was "papish" was therefore necessarily wrong. A number of the arts suffered from this feeling, but none more than sculpture and painting. Thousands of statues were overthrown and smashed, and thousands of pictures were destroyed or removed from churches, merely because of their association with Rome.

The other reason why paintings and statuary have not been in much favor among Protestants is the fear of idolatry. The Bible gives no encouragement whatsoever to the presence of images in churches. The Hebrews were not permitted to model, carve, or paint the human form or "make any graven image or any likeness of anything" for the purpose of worship. (Exodus 20:4.) And it was this prohibition more than any other factor which maintained their religion so much more pure and spiritual than those of the idolatrous nations around them. For the first three or four centuries of Christianity this same rule persisted; and then little by little, though the Church made frequent statements that they were for the purpose of veneration only, pictures and images were introduced.

Roman and Orthodox

IN THE Roman Catholic Church both paintings and statues are now in general use. Every church has on its walls the fourteen stations of the cross. These are pictures, or reliefs, representing scenes in the passion of our Saviour. They are arranged in chronological order, beginning with Jesus' condemnation by Pontius Pilate and ending with his being laid in the sepulcher. These stations, however, are not used in public devotions but rather in private prayer and meditation. Indulgences are granted for the people who pray before them. Churches usually also have statues of Jesus, of the Virgin Mary, of the patron saint of the church, and of various other saints. A Protestant, seeing people at prayer before these, is prone to denounce the practice as idolatry. Such prayer, though it may lead to idolatry and has real danger in it, may also be the sincere expression of the thoughts and feelings of a devout but simple-minded worshiper to God or to the mediating saint.

In every Roman Catholic Church, and in most Lutheran and many Episcopal churches, a crucifix, or cross bearing an image of Christ, is placed over the high altar. This usage was slow in arising and did not become universal until the Middle Ages; but it is by now thoroughly established in Roman churches. Among Episcopalians, although the majority still use the simple cross, the crucifix is growing in popularity. There are two sorts of crucifixes. One bears the figure of the dying or dead Christ, this cult having been popularized by medieval piety and carried on by the Jesuits. The other has the figure of the fully clothed, resurrected, victorious Christ. This style is more ancient than that of the "corpus," and is now slowly returning to favor.

In the Greek and Russian tradition, crosses are not very apparent in the churches. As among Roman Catholics, there are crosses on the outside of the buildings; and there is also a cross on every altar. However, the altar is hidden much of the time and there is only one altar in each church. On the altar cross is a painted representation of our Lord. Ever since the "iconoclastic controversy" of the eighth century no sculptured figure of the human body has been permitted by Orthodox law. Paintings, however, are not prohibited; they are exceedingly numerous in all churches. Many of these holy pictures comply with the law by presenting exposed parts of the human body (face and hands) in painted form only, but the halo, clothing, background, and framework in a sort of low relief, often in brass or even gold. Such a picture is called an icon.

The screen, or iconostasis, separating the sanctuary from the nave is lavishly hung with these icons. Surmounting the iconostasis there is often a cross, with a painted figure of Christ, in full view of the whole church. Before the Revolution in Russia icons were seen not only in churches but in railroad stations, post-offices, shops, living rooms of residences, at city street corners and in rural wayside shrines. They are greatly beloved by old-fashioned Russians, every devout Christian having his favorite icon. Orthodox church leaders, as do Roman Catholics, emphatically deny that these pictures are used as objects of worship. Worshipers are warned that while looking at the icons physically, they are to look mentally only upon Christ or his saints. Crosses in the East generally have two or three crossbars, the top one being supposed to have held the superscription, and the bottom one, often slanting, being that to which our Lord's feet were attached. The middle one is the longest.

Possibilities for Protestants

AMONG PROTESTANTS the plain symbol of the un-adorned cross seems to be quite sufficient to remind us of the death of Jesus. The realistic details of his pierced, bleeding hands, feet, and side, his thorn-matted head, his strained muscles, and his pain-distorted face, are not needed to produce in our souls a proper appreciation of his great love and sacrifice for us. Furthermore the cross should be, and surely is for most of us, a symbol of more than Jesus' suffering and death. It is a sign not only of his sacrifice but of his conquest, resurrection, and atonement; it stands for the historic and eternal Church, our whole religion, God himself; and it expresses our own willingness to live in the light and the spirit of these tremendous facts. When the figure of Jesus hangs upon it, the cross tends to be reduced in its imagery to merely one of its meanings, his passion and death. Hence the cross, if displayed at all in a Protestant church, ought to be plain. If possible it should be of gleaming metal, thus signifying not the rugged, realistic wood to which Jesus was nailed, but the eternal facts of sacrifice, victory, and redemption.

There are three reasons why it is more difficult for us to use

painting and sculpture as media for the expression of common
worship than it is to use words, music, drama, or dancing. The
first is the danger of idolatry or the fear of such a danger. The
second is that painting and sculpture are quite likely to be interpreted individualistically. Rather than uniting himself with
his fellow worshipers around a picture, each member of a group
is inclined to construe it for himself. The third is that pictures are
fixed, rather than fluid, in time. A painting is always the same,
whereas music and dancing are constantly changing, even as the
thoughts and moods of the human spirit change. Furthermore, in
painting and sculpture, as in all the arts, the danger of weakness
and sentimentality is always present.

Yet, in spite of difficulties involved, there assuredly are paintings which can unite men in their emotions and lead them to worship. Landscapes like those of Cézanne or of some of the great
Chinese masters may rise to such power, if given opportunity.
Whether these would be suitable for a church is doubtful but
many people would judge that provided they can release feelings
of group worship, they could be helpfully stationed before the
eyes of the people. Some Christmas pictures also have this power.
It is the opinion of the present writer that Giotto, of all the Christian artists, can probably best give expression to experiences of
united worship. Duccio, Simone Martini, Fra Angelico, Gerard
David, Jacopo Bellini, El Greco are other old masters who pos-
sessed a deeply devotional spirit, and whose works we can now
use.

Small, intimate groups can often worship by means of pictures
or statues if the conditions are right. Certainly these can do so
better than large groups can. The present tendency toward "worship centers" featuring pictures in Sunday schools and youth
rooms should be examined with great care. Though these "centers"
have certain advantages they also run risks. If the pictures are not
well chosen they may lead to sentimentalism rather than to power.
And even if the pictures are strong and expressive, they may di-
vide rather than unite the congregation because of personal differences in taste; or they may express but one aspect of the
complete worship experience. As individuals we can use pictures
for worship frequently; as small groups, sometimes; as large
groups, rarely.

Sculpture, for some mysterious reason, seems to come nearer to being socially expressive than painting. Perhaps this is because good sculpture in a church takes on an architectonic aspect. A good statue seems to belong in the place where it stands. Yet its place, like that of a picture, is rarely behind an altar or in any other central location. If it is weak or naturalistic in treatment, it detracts from the mystical feeling that should surround the table or the altar; and even if it is forceful and expressive, it will have the almost impossible burden of sustaining the complex totality of Christian experience. It is better to rely for this upon a simple cross with a curtain or paneled wooden background.

On side walls or over low doorways, under arches or in niches and recesses, pictures (whether murals or framed) and statues may be very helpful. Protestants will be learning ever more as time goes on to use churches and chapels for private worship. Roman, Orthodox, and Episcopal churches are constantly open for individual prayer and more and more this is also coming to be true of Protestant churches, especially in the cities. An individual who comes to worship alone in the church nave or in some chapel can be deeply moved to express his emotions through a great picture or statue. If a particular one does not help him, he does not have to pray before it. He can go to some other place in the church. Off-center wall spaces, or corners, or small chapels are consequently the most suitable places for whatever paintings and statues there may be. Many churches now have children's chapels, where pictures seem naturally to fit. But here as elsewhere we must beware of the fourfold dangers of sentimentalism, idolatry, divisiveness, and fixedness of mood.

Like stained-glass windows, pictures and statues should not be photographically realistic or primarily instructional. They should rely for the expressional effect upon form, color, design, inner life, and general emotional glow, rather than upon subject matter or detail. Too many pictures; pictures which do not fit into their architectural background or which disturb the harmonies of color and line; pictures whose composition is complicated or cluttered or whose technique is unskillful; pictures which direct the mind toward the glorification of the outer physical perfection rather than the inner attributes of the objects portrayed; and pictures which are striking or commanding of attention will more likely shatter the worshipful spirit than they will conserve or express it.

Symbolism in pictures and sculpture is an intricate study to which justice cannot of course be done in a few paragraphs. In the earliest Christian days it was often necessary for an author or artist to hide his real meaning from all eyes but those of the initiated. As time went on, although this necessity died out, symbolism was used to arouse emotions, to stir the imagination, to speak of values and virtues, to open up intricate philosophical speculations, or to identify saints.

The Nativity is a subject which has taken unto itself a wealth of such symbolism. The star, angels, the goldfinch, the apple, the grandiose but half-demolished stable in which Jesus was born, the Book—with the Infant pointing his finger to the prophecy of himself—the crown, often borne by angels, the blue of the mother's robe, the posture of her hands above the head of the Child, the presence of animals, saints, relatives, donors: all of these add excitement, imagination, and mystery to the simple Biblical tale. The Magi are generally three in number because of their association in men's minds with the three who refused to worship Nebuchadnezzar's image.

The Virgin is often seen seated on the throne of heaven, wearing a crown, or depicted in an enclosed garden, or at a well of living waters. She is shown with a star on her right shoulder, with the glory of the sun around her, or a crescent moon at her feet. She holds, or sits near, a lily or a rose. Or she clasps a sealed book as a sign that the meek possess the key to all wisdom.[3] In the hands of the infant Christ, a globe suggests his universal sovereignty, an apple the "Second Adam," the pomegranate hope and eternal life, the finch his soaring nature caged for a while in earthly form. In the pictures of the marriage of the Virgin, the story is often shown of the successful suitor's rod bursting into bloom as the sign that he is God's chosen one. In the death (or dormition) of the Virgin, the twelve apostles are gathered by a miracle to be present at the assumption. In her coronation, angels, patriarchs, prophets, apostles, martyrs, and church fathers may all be present regardless of their period in history.

St. John the Baptist is usually shown with a slim tall cross to

[3] Isaiah 29:11–19.

which is affixed a scroll: *Ecce Agnus Dei,* Behold, the Lamb of God. At his feet is a lamb. The four evangelists are all winged, signifying the speed of the Gospel's spread. The angel or winged man stands for Matthew, the winged lion for Mark, the winged ox for Luke, and the eagle for John. These figures are derived from the book of the Revelation. Each apostle has his own emblem or attribute. Peter has the keys, Paul a sword, Andrew an X-shaped cross, Philip a cross with a double bar, Batholomew the knife with which he was flayed, Judas Iscariot a money bag. Thomas has a builder's rule, illustrating the legend that Thomas, who was supposed to have gone to India, was paid by a king to build him a noble palace. Instead of erecting it, the apostle gave the money to the poor, and when reprimanded by the king, he replied that a palace had been built for him in heaven.

Other Biblical characters, the fathers of the Church, martyrs, heroes, missionaries, saints, angels, all have their own emblems. Some of them have a number of different emblems, and of course not all of these identifying marks appear in all of the paintings. The patron saint of a city or of a church often bears a model of that city or church in his hands. Cecilia plays an organ; St. Anthony of Padua holds the infant Jesus in his arms because the Infant once descended to comfort him; St. Augustine is shown with a pile of books at his feet; St. George with a sword and a shield, and often in the act of fighting the dragon; St. Nicholas, with three balls or three bags of gold which he tossed anonymously into the home of the poor but honest virgins who wished to be married. In order to enter fully and correctly into the artist's conception, one should be as cognizant as possible of the various symbols which have been traditionally used in the history of art.

It is assuredly dangerous to use pictures and statues in church. The Chinese Taoists, reduced from exalted spirituality to a debased superstition by their crass image worship, and some Roman Catholic Christians, with their naturalistic and wholly inadequate plaster casts, have amply proved that fact from different viewpoints. Many sensitive Catholics are now struggling against such false art. But if we are discriminate, aware of what we are doing, and well armored against idolatry, then let us not be afraid of the dangers! God gave us artists to help us to express our souls.

Let us, under the proper conditions and with sensible safeguards, welcome their aid.

Outside of Church

IT IS NOT ONLY in a church that a picture may be the vehicle of Christian feelings. We have all felt our hearts warmly stirred in the presence of certain masterpieces in museums, art shops, galleries, or private homes. A good picture or two in the narthex might very well greet the worshiper as he enters church, and another over the door cast a blessing as he leaves. A parish house might contain an informal and simple little art gallery. The church offices, Sunday-school rooms, scout rooms, parlors, and even social rooms, though perhaps not erected for the purpose of worship, nevertheless give people an opportunity to express their Christian lives. In the Sunday-school rooms, although worship experiences are to be kept always in mind, primary attention should be paid to the teaching element; in the social halls, to the decorative. Here therefore we can cheerfully admit historical illustrations, photographs, posters, and possibly even paintings which, though good, may not be by the greatest masters yet are adequate for their purpose of instruction or decoration. Wherever people go in the church house, let them be constantly aware of the fact that they are in a building set apart for Christian purposes, and let the artistic standards be high.

Another place where church art could be greatly improved is in our choice of Sunday calendars, Sunday-school cards, wedding and baptism certificates, and the like. One almost despairs on looking through the catalogues of many religious publishing houses and noting their wares. So many of the pictures express sentimentality and spiritual dry rot! If you ask these printers why they flood our churches with such easily purchasable and temptingly cheap standardizations they answer that they print what people like to buy! Consequently our only recourse is to broaden our knowledge and our taste and demand better products. Let us keep our Sunday calendars and our certificates very simple in their designs. It is better to have no pictures than poor ones. And on church calendars let the front page not speak of the minister, the choir or the janitor, but of God.

Our homes, too, ought to be the repositories for well-selected and highly expressive pictures. Real Christians want to show their Christianity. I once saw painted on the outside wall of a village residence in China, in great, bold, red letters, the words, "This is a Christian home." My heart was drawn to that house; and though I was just a passer-by I stopped off, introduced myself, and had Christian fellowship and prayer with its delightfully devout farmer family. Perhaps an American Christian home need not be so direct and conspicuous in its announcement; yet, if we recognize dignity and peace immediately upon entering it, should we not also be aware of its Christianity? Christianity is a very broad concept. Landscapes, still life, portraiture, flower designs, human figures, may all express the Christian spirit of their artists and owners even though they are not exclusively and indisputably Christian. We need not be narrow-mindedly theological or Biblical in our choices, but representations of good, wholesome, refined Christian thinking should be in evidence. Surely, too, we Christians ought to have somewhere in our homes our favorite picture of Jesus and some of our most beloved saints and teachers.

And What Is Greatness?

AND IF WE ARE striving in our souls to be great Christians why should we ever give way to an impulse to place in our churches, parish houses, or homes, pictures which are not great? Greatness is not just a matter of personal definition; if we do not know how to recognize greatness in paintings, we might well trust the judgment of the critics and display a few that they recommend, in order to see what unexpected stirrings these may let loose in our souls. In these days of printed color reproductions —the first age in man's history when we have been privileged to buy, cheaply, pictures so nearly like the originals that even artists can hardly tell them apart—there is little excuse for most of us not to have a few great pictures about us. Before buying them we should educate ourselves by paying frequent visits to

The Amiens School, about 1480: "The Last Supper." Many details are worthy of note, especially the little scene through the window at the right, of the Washing of the Disciples' Feet. (*Courtesy of the Art Institute of Chicago, Mr. and Mrs. M. A. Ryerson Collection.*)

Giotto: "The Presentation of the Child Jesus in the Temple," about 1305–1312. Although most of Giotto's works are frescoes, this one is on a wood panel. Joseph holds a pair of doves for the sacrifice as Simeon takes the Child in his arms, and Anna, a prophetess, comes in to be present at the event which her scroll has foretold. The background is of a rich gold, and the colors of the clothing are bright. (*Courtesy of the Isabella Stewart Gardner Museum, Boston*)

Giotto Workshop: "The Epiphany." The simplicity, sincerity, and humanity of Giotto and of his school appeal to all ages of Christians. (*Courtesy of the Metropolitan Museum of Art, New York*)

Fra Angelico, 1387–1455: "The Dormition and Assumption of the Virgin." Christ and the Apostles have gathered for the Virgin's death; in heaven there is triumph and ecstasy at her arrival. The baby held by Christ represents the soul of the Virgin whom Christ is receiving and will take up to heaven with him. Tempera, on wood. (*Courtesy of the Isabella Stewart Gardner Museum, Boston*)

Setting and characters for *Adam*, a mystery play of the twelfth century, translated by Edward Noble Stone, published by D. Appleton-Century Company, produced by the Department of Drama, Yale University. (*Courtesy of Yale University*)

Rhythmic choir in the Church of Christ, Hanover, New Hampshire, in Bortnian-sky's *Cherubim Song.* (*Courtesy of the Reverend and Mrs. Chester B. Fisk*)

William Blake (English) 1757–1827: "The Morning Stars Sang Together." A water color by an English mystic poet and painter. This is in a series of pictures on the Book of Job. Job and his wife and "comforters," are constrained in the earthly cave while God and his angels are full of rhythmic freedom above. (*Courtesy of the Pierpont Morgan Library, New Yrok*)

RIGHT. El Greco (Spanish), 1541–1614: "The Repentant Peter." The balanced design, the anguished expression, the elongation of the figure for the sake of emphasis are all characteristic of this artist. The keys are the emblem of St. Peter. (*Courtesy of the Phillips Memorial Gallery, Washington*)

BELOW. Rembrandt (Dutch) 1606–1669: "Christ Washing the Disciples' Feet." Dramatic lighting effects and the spiritual expression upon Christ's face, combined with the significant postures and faultless pattern of the disciples' figures, are the outstanding marks of this picture. (*Courtesy of the Art Institute of Chicago, Robert Alexander Waller Memorial Collection*)

André Derain, contemporary French, born 1880: "The Last Supper." A large picture, strong in concept, with simplest design and balanced masses, yet traditional in its groupings. Compare this to the elaborations and detail of

ABOVE. André Girard, born in France in 1901, was much influenced by his older friend, Rouault. This picture is one of a series of fourteen small panels of the "Stations of the Cross." Mother Mary is in turquoise blue, Christ in grey blue with a purplish red scarf, and the other figures in green. The effect is powerful. (*Courtesy of the Durand-Ruel Galleries, New York*)

LEFT. George Roualt, contemporary French, born 1871: "Christ and the Pharisee." Rouault's paintings are moving, elemental, with the glowing reds, blues, and greens, and the heavy outlines of stained glass. Serious, deeply in earnest, Rouault is one of the few great moderns who is a loyal churchman. (*Courtesy of the Phillips Memorial Gallery, Washington*)

Ernst Barlach: Monks Reading, 1932. Bronze, about two feet high. A superb example of modern architectonic sculpture. It should be in a church or in the library bay of some abbey. (*Courtesy of the Art Institute of Chicago, S. P. Avery Fund*)

Henry Moore, contemporary English: Madonna and Child, stone carving, detail, in St. Matthew's Church, Northampton, England. Born in 1898, Mr. Moore is probably the best known English sculptor at present. Many of his works are extreme in their modernism. This one has a strength and simplicity, yet popular comprehensibility, which have made it much beloved. (*Photographed by the sculptor; courtesy of Mr. Moore and* The Churchman, *New York*)

ABOVE. Charlton Fortune, contemporary American: "The Holy Family." This is a triptych used by the armed forces during the war. The restrained emotion, eagerness, yet boyish humility make this a much more satisfactory picture of the child Jesus than some which are better known. (*Copyright by Citizens Committee for the Army and Navy, Inc.*)

BELOW. Fred Nagler, contemporary American: "Without the Master." Mr. Nagler is an artist of experience and sincerity; many of his pictures are biblical and religious. This is an unusual subject. Every line, both in the figures and the mountains, signifies dejection. The Easter joy has yet to come. (*Courtesy of the Midtown Galleries, New York*)

ABOVE. Paul Cézanne (French) 1839–1906: "Saint Victoire Mountain." Cézanne is considered by many to be the founder of the modern school of painting. Detached, lonely, misunderstood, he revolted against the impressionists and sought for the solid, inward soul of his objects. (*Courtesy of the Metropolitan Museum of Art, New York*)

BELOW. Henry Mattson, modern American: "Wings of the Morning." There are a sweep and a creative power to this picture which stretch the spiritual imagination. (*Courtesy of the Metropolitan Museum of Art, New York*)

Tilman Riemenschneider (German), 1468?–1531: Head of St. John, from a large altar piece in the Herrgottskirche, Grelingen. Riemenschneider is the best known of the late medieval wood carvers. Though the austerity of earlier days seems to be retained in this head, one can see in much of Riemenschneider's work the beginnings of baroque fussiness and complexity. The clarity and simple lines of the twelfth and thirteenth century are now passing away. (*Photograph: Georg Scharfurt*)

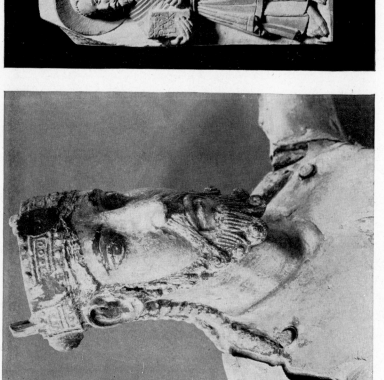

LEFT. Detail, Head of Christ, Spanish Romanesque crucifix, wood, 1150–1200. The elongated face helps bring out the emotion and reflects the strength of our own feelings. There is a quality in these medieval works for which many of the best of our sculptors today are seeking. (*Courtesy of the Cloisters, Metropolitan Museum of Art, New York*)

RIGHT. Limestone, Apostle Relief, Spanish, eleventh century. The more one studies these three figures the more of individuality and beauty one sees in them. The distortion, especially in hands and feet, is no doubt partly due to their original position over a doorway, which made the beholder view them from below. The fact that each one holds a tablet with his own name adds to the delightful naïveté of the group. (*Courtesy of the William Rockhill Nelson Gallery of Art, Kansas City*)

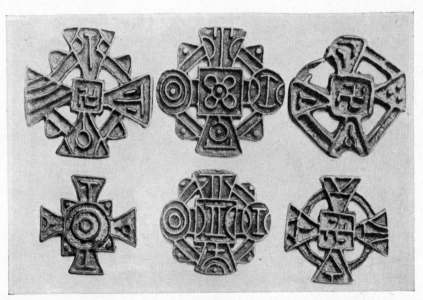

Bronze crosses and other figures, approximate size, probably from the thirteenth century. These are interesting remains found in a limited district in Mongolia about the year 1920. Several thousand of them have been discovered. Though nothing can be proved as to their origin, it is known that the area where they were found was once inhabited by a Nestorian tribe; one can easily note symbols which may be Christian: the fish, the dove, the triangle, the Tau Cross, the Pi (possibly the Greek initial of *Pater,* father) the I (possibly for Jesus), the swastica, the three balls, the quatrefoil, the concentric three circles, and the characteristic Nestorian cross, shaped much like the Maltese. (*From the Collection of the Reverend and Mrs. Mark Brown*)

The Church of St. John

Let all mortal flesh keep silence and ponder within itself no earthly thing for the King of kings and Lord of lords cometh. ⊔⊔·⊔⊔·

Alleluia! Alleluia! Alleluia! Lord Most High!

Design for the Front Cover of a Church Calendar, by the Reverend Sam T. Lenters.

museums and galleries, reading good modern books, and subscribing to an art magazine or two. We might also consult our local high-school teacher or museum director. On the whole it is best to study, think, and then to act on our own judgment. In the meanwhile, let us beware of the over-commercialized popular pictures of the day. Hofmann, Holman Hunt, and Sallman seem to be the ones the publishers wish us to buy just now. Be careful! For though these have virtues, they hardly stand the tests of greatness.

True art does not seek to reproduce on canvas that which the artist sees with his outward eye. It is not imitative or photographically representative of the outer object. An artist paints his own soul, his inner reactions to certain external facts. If his soul is great, and if his skill is adequate, then the result is great. If it is objected that this seems to reduce an artist's work too entirely to the subjective, one would reply that the artist while painting does not think much about himself at all. He concentrates not upon his soul, but upon the object before him, and seeks to enter appreciatively into its spirit. Then he paints whatever comes naturally out of his soul at the moment. The object generates in him a thought or an emotion; it is this thought or emotion that he expresses.

Although the artist depicts himself, he is not unduly introspective or self-conscious. He merely has the urge to express his own reactions as they are when he is confronted by some stimulating fact outside of himself. If, however, it is the reactions of his group that he is seeking to set down, he must be somewhat more socially analytical than if he simply externalizes his own personal reactions. A few artists have so completely identified themselves with the group-soul that they can express complex states of living with ease.

To a certain extent all artists express more than just their own selves. They live in traditions, schools, countries, cultures, eras, religions; and they can hardly help being part of these surroundings. With enough study in history any one of us could state approximately out of what age and land almost any given picture has come. Very few pictures can step completely out of their environments and be completely individualistic. Nevertheless it is harder to give natural, simple, and straightforward expression to a group feeling than it is to a personal feeling. An artist who can identify himself with a great-souled group and express that group's noblest and deepest reactions to life or to God is a greater artist than one who speaks only for himself. This is a rare attainment.

A great work of art is one which gives adequate outward expression to an inner experience of the artist or his group when they have been deeply stirred by communion with some part of the natural or spiritual world. Great Christian art is the expression, through any given medium, of such an experience on the part of a great Christian. Great church art is art which gives expression to a profound experience of a body of Christians in the conscious presence of God, in church.

We Moderns

FOR A LONG TIME the Western world has been under the spell of the school of naturalistic realism in art; so much so, indeed, that if one asks the average person what the chief function of a picture is he will probably answer that it is to reproduce, as nearly as possible within the limits of the medium chosen, the actual object pictured. If it succeeds in this, it is considered to be a good picture; if not, it is a bad one.

When we come to think it over, there is nothing very creative about this. When we listen to a sermon or read a book, we do not merely accept every word of it and seek to remember it verbatim. Rather we set our minds to work upon it, selecting and emphasizing; we discard one thought, enlarge upon another, and perhaps violently disagree with a third. In doing so we become creative thinkers in regard to the book we have read or the sermon we have heard.

So it is with an artist and a natural object. Given a landscape, a sunset, a house, the body of an animal or a human being, the stable at Bethlehem, Jesus at Emmaus, a saint, a factory, an engine, an arrangement of fruits, or the contents of a business man's desk-top, the creative artist will immediately begin to organize, distort, eliminate, and emphasize. The object need not have intrinsic beauty to arouse him to creation. The artist wants not to reproduce but to create; not to re-express actions but to express reactions.

There must be first, however, an object, of which the artist is fully aware. Some artists of recent years have attempted to get along without objects at all. The straight lines and colored rectangles of Mondrian, and the non-objective paintings of many others, are probably but a passing fad. So, also, are the other extremes of modernism, such as cubism, surrealism, and Dadaism.

But the artists of the last generation or so have nevertheless hit upon a truth which most of our ancestors since Rembrandt seem to have forgotten: that it is the internal reaction rather than the external object that is of supreme importance. I looked through a series of reproductions of the British Royal Academy from 1893–1903 recently, and was amazed to see how almost totally unsatisfactory they are as works of art. A large number of them seek to tell stories, a task much more fitly left to the author than to the painter. Others try to glorify nature, or the simple country life, or England, or a starchy aristocrat, or the army, or the Church, or some Greek goddess, or virtue in general. Practically all of them, whether painting or statue, make the most meticulous efforts to reproduce every last flower, whisker, and fingernail, in all their natural precision.

Now there is a place for this natural precision, but that place is in photography, not in painting or modeling. Photography, and the photographic school of painting, have a legitimate function in the world of education. To teach a boy or girl just how Jesus dressed, ate, and worked at his carpenter's bench is an excellent enterprise. Our Sunday-school libraries should surely contain pictures by Tissot and other historically accurate Bible illustrators, and also modern prints and photographic slides, and motion-picture films of Bible customs.

Nor do I mean, either, to be disrespectful to photographers as artists. Many of them are artists as fully as painters. They start with an object, as painters do; but by means of the arrangement of lights, the use of filters, and the application of different types of developing and printing, these artist-photographers bring to the surface their own reactions. They select, hide, minimize, distort, and emphasize. In other words, though they must remain within the limits of their medium, still they do seek within those limits to do just what a painter, engraver, woodcarver, or sculptor seeks to do. There is a real difference between the artist-photographer and the commercial or educational photographer.

But to return to painting: a good picture does not seek to reproduce a given object in all its details. It is the inner experience of the artist himself that we must look for in any work of art. There is in a great picture a vitality, a glow of life, a spiritual quality, and an intensity of feeling, which lies underneath yet mysteriously seems contained in the outer form which the painting takes. In addition to its own distinctive laws, the basic canons of unity, design, rhythm, balance, clarity, and simplicity are operative in painting as in the other arts.

In sculpture, additional features for which we look are firmness, solidity, weightiness. We find an awareness of rocklike monumentality, a sense of a statue's having grown up out of its own base, or a feeling of its belonging exactly to its environment. Statues, like stained-glass windows, and even more than pictures, often have distortions of anatomy or clothing when they are designed to be viewed at a distance or from a lower level. Exterior smoothness, gracefulness, plausibility, scientific naturalism, and historical accuracy are no more to be sought for in statues than in pictures. Plaster casts are almost always fragile looking, for plaster is not the right medium for sculpture. Wood, bronze, terra cotta, are all excellent media, although many prefer stone. The new science of plastics has some interesting possibilities to offer the sculptor, but it will be long before this medium attains discipline.

Our Heritage

HISTORY HAS SEEN but a limited number of really great pictorial artists. Some in the very childhood of the race, uninhibited by conventions or by efforts to please an art-buying public, produced peculiarly true art. The caves of Altamira were decorated by painters of the first rank. The Aztecs and Mayas also did much work which rates high. Many early Chinese and Indian artists were truly great; the Chou dynasty bronzes have rarely been surpassed. Cretan art; Greek art before the days of its Hellenistic decline; Byzantine art; Gothic art before it became flamboyant; late medieval and Renaissance paintings before the refinements of Raphael; the Han and T'ang productions in China before the Sung impressionists; and certain individuals of the late Rennaisance (El Greco, Tintoretto, Rembrandt, Michelangelo, and later, Blake) had the knowledge, the skill, and the depth of soul to be really great expressionists. At no time in Europe between the so-called "primitives" of the late Middle Ages and the so-called "moderns" (beginning with Cézanne) of the nineteenth and twentieth centuries, has there been a whole school which satisfies the critics of today.

The modern, like the medieval, artists have made a significant discovery. They are not to be laughed off as childish because of their distortions and bright colors; nor as careless and ignorant because of their uncouth figures or rough outlines. On the other hand, no artist is to be considered great simply because he is "modernistic." Time will winnow for us the worthy from the unworthy. On the whole the moderns are on the right track, and after the excesses of the revolution have worn off it is hoped that we shall accept forms which will free us from the comfortably deadening smoothness of the imitative naturalists.

Christians, as we examine our heritage, find ourselves in an exceedingly fortunate situation. Many of the greatest artists of our civilization have been earnestly Christian. The Byzantines, Giotto, Duccio, Fra Angelico, the Van Eycks, Memling, some miniature illustrators, and the early Gothic sculptors, sought first of all to give expression to their own Christian experience; and their Christianity was highly ecumenical. Today we are in a better position to appreciate and understand these greatest ones of the past than were our Victorian grandfathers.

Of very recent years there has been a revival of interest in Christian painting, even among some of our extreme modernists. Charlot, Derain, Rouault, Chagall, Beckmann, Hartley, and even Picasso are producing religious pictures that are certain to survive their age. In sincerity and humility, and even with strength and a wealth of skill, these present-day Christians are seeking to express the intensities and the tragedies of our times. The passion and crucifixion of our Lord are the subjects to which they return again and again. Why should the Church not use these artists more, to the glory and worship of God?

CHAPTER IX

The Artist Himself

~~~~~~

EVEN A CHILD is to some extent an artist. For every child engages in play; and creative play conforms to the rules of art. A small boy, "playing horse," has seen the object, horse; he has entered into such a pleased relationship with it that he even assumes for himself certain qualities of "horsiness"; and then he gives expression to this feeling of horsiness by trotting, galloping, neighing, or pulling a wagon. A girl with her dolls goes through much the same process. So does every adult, in countless situations, almost every day of his life, though the objects which attract him, and his relationship and reactions to them, are quite different.

Perception

BEING CREATIVE involves awareness of the existence of something outside ourselves. This quality is universal; every one of us is aware of many objects. Yet it is obvious, too, that no one perceives all that he might. How many things there are which, seeing, we see not, and hearing, we hear not! These objects range from the majesty of God down to the shine on the head of many a pin. The stars in their nightly splendor; the changing colors of a blowing tree; the precision of angular relationships inside a circle; the gleam of the sunlight on one's arm still wet from swimming; the expression of serene benevolence in some old woman's face—these we too often let pass unnoticed.

The alternative is not to go about tingling over and over to the glory of every stamen of every flower. Our nerves would not stand it. We can train ourselves to observe beauties without loss of natural tranquillity. Elizabeth Goudge tells, in one of her novels, about a Chinese bowl which was in the possession of an English family. For years it had stood on its table in the hallway largely unheeded, until one day it was broken, "when they suddenly remembered that it had been priceless." [4] Yet the very fact that they had "suddenly remembered" indicates that, in some mysterious way, they had been noticing it all along. Its grace, colorfulness, and symmetry had subtly been making their marks on the souls of those people; and now when it was gone they missed it. The creative person lives in such a way that outer objects are either consciously observed or subtly absorbed into his consciousness.

Sight, hearing, and the other senses are not the only means by which we receive impressions. In the mysterious workings of our inner lives we often become aware of things too deep for the senses to perceive. William Penn said of Fox that "he was a discerner of others' spirits." So, too, are some people discerners of the living God. To those who do not perceive these glories they seem not to exist. To those who do become aware of them, they are the very stuff of life itself.

Relationship

AGAIN, BEING CREATIVE involves not only an awareness of the existence of outer objects but also a subtle sort of relationship with them. There is a give and take between them and us. At least this is true as far as our relationships with other human personalities and with God are concerned. Even inanimate articles have a decided influence upon us and are subject to our own choice or rejection. The qualities of the buildings in which we live, work, study, and worship cast their sway over us in ways of which we are not always conscious. At times this is for good; at times, no doubt, for bad. Sometimes we become aware of bad influences and rebel against them; often we just succumb to evil charms without even admitting their spell. A church, for example, with a quarrelsome head end, its lines all broken up by organ pipes, chairs, light fixtures, disorderly music racks, inharmonious colors, and garish wall designs, tends to insinuate its character

[4] *The Castle on the Hill,* Coward-McCann, Inc., p. 292.

into our own unless we revolt. Many times such a church building has been deeply loved from childhood because of its associations and therefore is still thought beautiful by the people who worship there Sunday by Sunday. They publicly confess an affinity for it, do not like to hear it criticized, resist all efforts to change it. Preference has its roots in personal experiences and argument will rarely prevail against it.

Taste does however frequently change and develop. This change takes place not by frontal effort but rather when that which we are trying to express is found to be too profound for the old accustomed forms to externalize. If we have inside of us thoughts and feelings which are essentially Christian, then we shall strive to find ever more satisfactory means of giving them outer manifestation. We shall be on the search for a better type of architecture or music or drama or poetry or decorational design than we have been employing hitherto. We shall be asking about forms which appeal to other people. We shall go visiting other churches, looking at pictures, reading books on ecclesiastical architecture. As we engage in these processes our taste will inevitably change. We may call this a change for the better if it gives us ampler opportunity to bring out into the open the thoughts and feelings which seemed "cabin'd, cribb'd and confin'd" within the inadequate forms to which we had been inured.

Some people, to be sure, never outgrow their original environment. It may be that the difficulties in certain situations really are too great to be overcome; or it may be that the minds and feelings of these particular persons are not big enough to want to search for wider roads. If our feelings seem fenced in by such old wonted forms, then what we most need is to jump fences and take up with the new! Generally these new appreciations will come gradually. One cannot expect suddenly to shift from comics to Michelangelo, from crooning to Beethoven, from jingles to Walt Whitman, from a horror motion picture to Shakespeare. Yet once liberated from childish forms, we fairly shout with the joy of being able really to express what we had thought inexpressible.

Appreciation is entering eagerly but humbly into an intimate relationship with some person or object and searching for the new life to be found therein. It is willingness to learn all there is to learn about things both new and old. It is studying the laws of their nature. The more we learn about how a certain picture has been constructed—why its lines were made to go this way or that, why this particular color or that particular material was chosen, how this plane was used to balance that void—the more we shall enjoy it. The more we enjoy it, the more we can entrust it with the responsibility of expressing the deepest things of our minds and spirits.

Adoration is standing in wonder before God's greatness, majesty, and glory. Full adoration does not ordinarily come with one cursory glance or one flash of astonishment. It grows with the study of the laws by which God reveals himself to men. The application of the mind to the ways by which the universe behaves—how light, sound, electricity, chemicals, the human body, atomic energy, conduct themselves and carry on their work—can be a clear road toward the adoration of God. So also can Bible reading, and the love of all kinds of art. Our ability to adore is measured by our experience and our knowledge. If we know but little of God or experience him but dimly, we can adore him but feebly. The more we learn of him from all possible sources, the more we are lost in his praise.

Art, in this phase of its definition, is the relationship in which we live with the external factors in our environment. Taste is our choice of the objects with which we wish to have deeper and continuing relationships. Appreciation is entering fully into the beauties and joys of those objects which our taste has chosen. The only limit to either good taste or high appreciation is the greatness of our own soul. If our soul is great it spurs us constantly on to find more and more fitting outer objects and forms by which to manifest ourselves externally.

Expression

THE CREATIVE PERSON, besides perceiving and appreciating, must do something in response. He must speak, paint, write, sing, dance, work, or pray. He must get his emotions out into the open by means of some significant form, whether just for private joy or as a means of communication with other people. All of us, of course, are doers and all have some skills. We talk, we sew, we garden, we play tennis. Who has not seen a woman arranging her hair over her ears or smoothing out her dress after she has crossed her knees? These are skillful acts. So are the acts of good moral living. Skill and creativeness are needed in one's daily occupation, whether as machinist, farmer, carpenter, barber, lawyer, teacher, or mother. We all engage in many "practical" arts, without labeling them arts. Yet in addition to these necessary arts or skills we also ought to cultivate some "fine" art, art for its own sake, art which many people would call just waste of time. This is one of the most enjoyable and soul-fulfilling functions in which man can engage. To be whole men we must also be creative in our acts merely for the sake of creating.

Forming an "Arts Guild"

WE CAN BE creative artists alone if we will, experimenting with many means until we come upon something that "strikes fire." A studio or workshop in the cellar is a wholesome addition to any home. One can subscribe to several good journals giving precise information as to where and how to purchase materials, how to begin, and what pitfalls to avoid. Any friend who has recently begun will be glad to pass on hints, as will the clerks in the supply stores. Do not hesitate to tell them you are a beginner; they will know it anyway. You will find it simple in these days to get instruction through art schools, colleges, extension courses, adult education centers, summer camps, or by mail. You may even discover, much to your own surprise, that you are talented, and decide to enter art as a life work. The varieties of art to which one may apply himself these days, both professional and commercial, are extraordinary. Dress designing, tile-making, weaving, engraving, embossing, the painting of tin trays, are only a few that jump to mind. The field will open enormously once you get into it.

Most beginners, however, having little time or desire for lonely experimentation, will want the encouragement of working with others as they learn. If there is already one in your neighborhood, you can join a local hobby group or guild and find both satisfaction and fellowship in it. You may also be interested to learn of a new movement known as the "Arts Guild," which has already been established in the Congregational Christian churches. A similar or branch organization may be started anywhere. Let us examine how such a self-organized local unit would operate.

An Arts Guild is more than just a hobby group in a church. It is a companionship, giving artistic expression to Christian impulses and Christian ideals. A typical group consists of about ten men and women who meet in a church parsonage. First they unite their spirits in worship, adoring God, giving him hearty thanks for all his own infinite artistry in nature, and dedicating to him the work of the evening. Then there is a period of appreciation, when some picture is exhibited, discussed, and analyzed; or when some member of the group displays his own collection of prints; or when the librarian of the town gives a short talk on what books are locally available; or when a brief and elementary course in the history of church art is led by the minister; or when one's own church is examined to see how it might be improved in its worshipful qualities; or when phonograph records of great church music are played. The opportunities for the period of appreciation are endless, and the danger is that this period will lap over into the next period, which is that of creation.

For the creative period the group retires to the cellar, where a workbench or easels go well with the queer smocks or inverted bathrobes which the members now don. Here for an hour or more each one experiences the fascination of creating. Perhaps all will choose to unite in a single project, everyone engaging, for example, in water-color painting. Or perhaps each one will follow his own specialty—pencil sketching, lettering, embroidery, dressmaking, linoleum block printing, wood carving, or bookbinding. Some people will want to do nothing but give vent to their own personal urges or follow their own impulses. Perhaps they will make birthday cards, handkerchiefs, or mantel ornaments for private use.

A local high-school teacher is generally to be found who is willing to give of her time voluntarily as a coach. The coach will give suggestions on how to buy materials and how to proceed in the activities, portioning her attention from pupil to pupil. The cost of material used by individuals should be borne by themselves but the group also might own some equipment in common and all ought to contribute to pay the expenses of the coach.

It is to be expected that, among other things, a Christian will sometimes, at least, paint or otherwise fashion a very definitely Christian object; such as a wooden cross, or some saint, or the manger scene, or an Easter card. How could a Christian stay completely away from such objects as these? An individual in the group might very well feel the urge to make something for the church: an embroidered altar cloth, a design for the weekly calendar, an offering plate, a children's name roll for the primary room, a poster for a party, some flowerpots for the dining room. A minister might make his own wedding certificates in careful hand lettering or a Sunday-school superintendent his own promotion cards.

Any articles made for church use or to represent the church before the public should always be submitted anonymously, through the president of the Guild, to the art committee of the church for approval or rejection. Let no one submit such a contribution without being told beforehand to be quite prepared for its rejection and if he is not willing to accept the verdict in good spirit let it not be submitted. This is essential to maintain the public standards of the church.

The Guild may decide to disclose its group feelings by projecting a rough outline for a new chancel, or making recommendations for the refurnishing of a certain room in the church building. The Guild ought to have influence in raising the artistic culture of the whole membership of the church. It will only be by ordinary people taking extraordinary interest in such matters that a matrix will be formed out of which, perhaps in the not too far distant future, first-rate artists for the Church will be born. It is from folk art that professional art arises.

Such articulations on the part of Christian people can release many pent-up emotions, ease nervous strains, and aid in general health. Study will be encouraged, and this will deepen their knowledge and appreciation of the Church as an ongoing historic organization; teach them much about the general culture of mankind; develop their sense of tolerance of others' tastes and ideas; and afford true Christian fellowship and inner satisfaction.

Many mature Christians will also see the appropriateness of seeking to express their political, economic, and social ideals through artistic efforts. Although we must admit that anxiety for a better world does not invariably keep company with the fine arts, nor even with prayer and worship, for that matter, there is a genuine tendency toward an alliance between these two aspects of life. A sincere artist, like a sincere worshiper, looking at life as a whole and seeking to have relationship with all of its parts and personalities, tries to bring whatever reactions grow out of his life-view into overt expression. It is unbelievable that a desire to improve the status of the Negro, for instance, will not result in an earnest effort to depict sympathetically the soul of any individual Negro with whom a given white man has come into contact. The same can be said of a concern for justice in industry, improvement in housing and city planning, production of better manufactured articles, educational equality, international friendship, or other Christian ideals. On the other hand, the more such hopes are artistically expressed, the more will they be strengthened, and unconsciously translated into practical service. An Arts Guild can give expression to the social ideals of a local church by composing special liturgical, dramatic, or pictorial material for Labor Day, patriotic days, international peace days, missionary meetings, social-action services, or other occasional ceremonies. Creative art can thus serve a real purpose in giving voice to the social conscience of a Christian community.

Training in the development and expression of our social thoughts and emotions through artistic creation is one of the urgent needs of our age. If this point were made clear to men in general, it would quite possibly result in a rapid return both to artistic efforts within the Church and to common worship. An Arts Guild in a local church, though at first glance it may not seem to have much relationship to the problems and complexities of modern living, is therefore, if properly conceived and dedicated, a very practical thing. Yet its usefulness will not come by a strained effort to improve the world, but rather as a by-product of the urge to self-expression on the part of a company of people who have a thoroughly Christian social attitude. This is a very different thing from propaganda.

Every church has now at least one group which might be called an Arts Guild—the choir. Some also have drama guilds. But other arts than music and drama could be employed in the same wholesome, happy, and useful way. Indeed it is not too much to hope that before long churches may have "ministers of art" in somewhat the same way in which they now have ministers of music. A man or woman who can lead in the musical development of the church might also be capable of leading in these other ways that have been suggested. Thereby the whole life and worship of the church would be stimulated and given beneficial and exhilarating representation.

The Great Goal

CHRISTIAN ART MAY be an expression on the part of any single Christian, representing himself alone; or it may be the expression of an individual who consciously seeks to sum up in his work the whole Christian ideal; or it may be the group expression of a limited Christian company working together on some project; or it may be, in some mysterious way, the expression by all of us Christians together of the whole historic, world-wide Christian genius and tradition. No liturgy or hymn or prayer, no building or style of architecture, no single picture or school of painting, no one creed or social attitude has as yet risen to become an adequate expression of universal and timeless Christian thought and feeling.

There are, however, several things which in themselves do approximate an expression of the whole. One is the celebrations of the church year, particularly Advent, Christmas, Lent, Good Friday, Easter, Pentecost. Another is the Bible, that unique work of art which gives expression to the combined Christian faith and feeling of us all. Another is the Church—not any one denomination but the Holy Catholic Church. For the Church is a supernal work of art. It was formed by men, under God's guidance, as a response to the overwhelming recognition of God's presence and continues to live in his fellowship. It comes from the heart not of any one man or any one nation or any one group but of Christian men and women as a whole; and in spite of its divisions, its frequent intolerances, and obvious faults, the Church is a continuing symbol of the united Christian soul.

By the Church we bind ourselves together into a fellowship of sympathy and love. In the Church we study and are instructed in the ways and means of Christian living. Through the Church we serve those who are in need. By means of the Church we unite in worship before Almighty God, our Creator and Father and the God and Father of our Lord Jesus Christ.

For a Christian, worship is the fundamental act of living. We recognize and acknowledge God to be our Lord; we adore him and enter upon a series of relationships with him; and we act before him in ways of praise, confession, petition, intercession, thoughtful reflection, and sacrifice. Out of worship comes everything that is worth while. As theology used to be called the Queen of the Sciences, so can worship be called the Queen of the Arts. For it includes all other arts, directing them toward God. Worship is the touchstone for all our perceptions, relationships, and actions, to see if they be in tune with the highest. Without worship a Christian would have nowhere to point his life. With it, everything he does has an adequate reason for being, and every impulse is impelled to express itself greatly.

Then let all Christians together, with all our hearts and all our minds and all our skills, express ourselves in earnestness and devotion to the God who made and loves us and who delights in our response.

Questions for the Reader

~~~~~~

I

WHERE ART BEGINS

What is your definition of art? Compare it with the definition this book favors.

What is the chief function of art? Is there danger of overstressing the subjective aspect of expression?

Do people have a right to expect of an artist that he reproduce as closely as possible, in his own medium, some natural object?

Should art be concerned always with the beautiful? Why "waste time" painting an object that is not beautiful?

Must art always be understandable by those who see it or hear it?

Name some arts which are not mentioned in this chapter.

What is the difference between the "fine" arts and the "useful" arts? Is this a valid distinction?

What is meant by the phrase "art for art's sake"? Do you agree with its implications?

What is your definition of Christian art? Is your definition more concerned with impression or expression?

How would you distinguish between Christian art and general religious art?

Can a non-Christian artist lead Christians in sincere worshipful expression?

Should everything that does not lead the group in worship be excluded from a church?

Can nonchurch art ever be a means of worship?

Must all church art be social in its expression? (That is, the expression of a group mind?)

II

THE ART OF COMMON WORSHIP

Must we have some experience of God before we can worship?

What is your definition of worship? Can worship properly be called an art?

Should worship be for its own sake, or is there some ulterior aim for which we should strive?

Is God outside of ourselves or within? Or both? Do we worship Jesus, or God only? Did Jesus die for us? Is the chief revelation of God to be found in the Bible? On the answer to these and other such questions depends much of our philosophy of worship. How would such differences of theology assert themselves in methods of worship?

What are the underlying unities between Jewish and Christian worship? Between Roman Catholic and the various kinds of Protestant worship?

What are the chief differences? Are these superficial or fundamental?

Is there any value in establishing the "fact" (as many denominations seem desirous of doing) that our own type of worship is in truth the New Testament type?

What are the most important contributions to worship of the Eastern, Roman Catholic, Lutheran, Anglican, Presbyterian, Free Church, Friends, Seventh Day Adventist, Pentecostal, Salvation Army groups?

What is the essential difference between the "high church" and the "low church" traditions?

What are the differences between the "Word of God" service and the "Upper Room" service?

Why is it that most Protestants use the latter so much less often than the former? What do you think of the proposition that we hold communion service every Sunday?

Is there a natural order, or sequence, of worship moods? What is it? If this order is not followed, is something essential lost?

Is there a natural order, or sequence, in the communion service?

Name, in the order of their importance, all of the chief aspects of the Lord's Supper. Is it true that they can be reduced to the two basic elements of sacrifice and communion? Of these two which does your own church stress the more? Rightly?

How could the order of service in your church be improved to include all the basic elements of worship in the proper order? How could it be improved in the materials of worship used?

Is it true that the average American Protestant finds the service dull because there is not enough for him to do and to see? If so, how rectify the situation?

III

The Church Building

Can a person worship God just as well in a barn as in a cathedral?

Do you think that any one style of architecture is more religious than any other style? More Christian? Why?

What is your opinion of "modernistic" style? What are the moderns trying to do? Is it suitable for churches?

Remembering that the eye naturally follows a line, which kind of line—vertical or horizontal, straight, crooked, or gracefully curved—is the most likely to lead the mind to God? Why?

Is a dome in itself religious? Is a cruciform ground plan?

Is beauty necessarily a religious quality?

Is a steeple a sign of a grandeur complex? What right has a Christian church to spend money on such "unessentials" when people are starving?

What share does the church bell have in a service of worship?

Should a church be the proper size to accommodate the largest annual congregation or the average weekly congregation?

What is the effect of a gallery on the people who sit in it? On the minister and choir?

What are the advantages or disadvantages of sloping floors, theater chairs, curved pews, carpets, cushions, hassocks, sliding walls?

What are the differences between good and bad stained glass? What shall we do with the bad glass in our church? Or, if nothing can be done about it now, how shall we prevent its repetition?

Criticize the phrase "dim, religious light."

Do you prefer visible light fixtures or indirect lighting? Why?

According to what principles should trees and shrubs be arranged on the church grounds?

What rules would you lay down for exterior bulletin boards and interior hymn boards?

IV

Fittings and Furniture

Does a church architect have to be Christian? Is it not enough that he know what is beautiful and leave the Christianity to the worshipers?

Put into as few words as you can what a "functional" church building is.

Is it true that if a church is functional it will inevitably tend also to
be beautiful? If so, then why is it that our very earnestly Christian
grandparents so often produced such ugly church architecture?

Describe the differences between the arrangements, furniture, and
symbols of the main Protestant denominations.

Are these differences the expressions of radically different tempera-
ments, or do most people just thoughtlessly accept the tradition in
which they have been brought up?

Why is it that most people become so attached to their own customs
that even minor changes often irritate them acutely? What value
is there in tradition?

What is a symbol? Why is a symbol so powerful emotionally?

What symbols in your church building make it unmistakably a church
(in distinction to a theater, concert hall, Y.M.C.A. auditorium)?

Discuss the relative merits of altar and table; of divided choir and a
choir facing the congregation; of central pulpit and central table;
of central and side aisles. Give reasons why the cross should or
should not be used as an agent of church worship.

Is it idolatry to treat the communion table with such respect that
notebooks, hats, and other objects are not allowable on it even when
church is not in session?

Give reasons why a cross should be on the pinnacle of a church. Or,
why it is not so suitable there as a weather vane.

The Church being an international institution, is there any place in it
for a national flag? If so, what is its function? What placement best
fulfills this function?

What are the fundamental rules for flower arrangement in church?
How do these rules differ from those for flower arrangement in the
home?

Do color, design, and "atmosphere" in a department store affect your
"sales resistance"? Does light have an influence on the output of
factory workers? Which colors act in which ways for you?

What do you think of the color scheme for church worship as out-
lined by the author? Is it mere fancifulness, or has it real religious
value?

Why do Protestant ministers so often wear black? What emotions does
this express? When you honestly think it over, would you not
prefer them to be somewhat brighter in their clothing? (Remember
that it was only "the day before yesterday" that most Protestant
ministers wore street clothes in church, and elaborate Eucharistic

vestments are comparatively recent even among Episcopalians.)
Why is this change of attitude coming toward vestments?

Should anyone who wishes to do so have the right of placing a
memorial tablet in church in honor of some loved one? Who should
make the decision? And who should decide upon the design?

How would you go about rearranging the architecture and furniture
of your own local church in order to help it to express your moods
of worship?

What are the values in the church year?

V

THE ART OF MUSIC

Is music natural to Christian worship? Is it necessary?

What is the fundamental purpose of music in church? Is this purpose
the same in instrumental music as in vocal? In choral as in congregational?

Is there anything naturally religious or Christian about any one type
of music? Or irreligious about another?

Why do you suppose it is that congregational hymn singing is so nearly
universal among Protestants and so nearly nonexistent among Roman
Catholics?

What values do we Protestants thus have which our Catholic friends
miss?

Distinguish between a great composer and a great Christian composer.
Place the well-known composers in the order of their greatness, according to your opinion. Which of these seem to you to be Christian?

What are the qualities that make an anthem great? A hymn tune?
An organ voluntary?

Should we, in our church worship, confine ourselves to great music
only?

Why is it that Victorian hymns are not admired by the "high-brows"?
Shall we ignore the "high-brows" or seek to discover what they are
driving at?

What shall a minister do about hymns which his congregation demands but which he himself, from his study and experience, knows
are not able to express what the congregation can and would like
to express?

What should a congregation do if its minister chooses hymns that the
congregation deems unworthy?

How many hymn tunes do you think you know by heart? How many

do you think you could know? Compare hymn tunes with hymn
   words in this respect.
How long would it take the average public-school graduate to learn
   a new, relatively simple hymn if he really tried?
Is it true that there are some people who can just never learn to carry
   a tune?
How do the arrangements of the seats in the choir affect congrega-
   tional worship? The placement of the organ pipes? Of the console?
In what ways other than its singing may the choir have an influence,
   for good or bad, over congregational worship?
Name some practices in choirs which may be called "show-off."
Why is choral music, on the average, considered to be better in
   churches than quartets, duets, and solos? Do you agree?
To what Christian test would you put a candidate for membership in
   a choir?
What are the values of congregational participation in choral amens,
   introits, chants, responses?

VI

Church Literature

Why should we stick to the King James Version when new transla-
   tions may be more accurate and almost as beautiful?
Does the Bible always have to be read in church? Cannot some
   modern poetry or other selection be substituted for it?
Or if the Bible be insisted upon, why, at any rate, so much of the
   Old Testament?
On what principle should selections from the Bible be chosen for the
   comparatively few readings which may be given in the course of
   the year?
What are the arguments for and against responsive readings?
What is the root meaning of "introit"? (It might be wise, by the way,
   to look up the pronunciation of this word.) What forms may the
   introit take?
What is the value of a call to worship? Or to attend to Bible reading,
   or to prayer, or offertory, or to the listening to announcements? Or of
   an ascription after sermon? Should we "clutter up" the service with
   such "extras" and "interruptions"?
Does sincere prayer always come from the heart rather than from a
   book?
Why bother the congregation to join in unison or responsive prayers,
   when the minister could say the prayer for everyone?

Should "Amen" always be sung after a hymn? Or said after a prayer?

Which are of more importance in a hymn: words or music?

Is the sermon an act of worship on the part of the congregation or not?

Make a list of the Christian reading that you have done during the past year. How did you distinguish between what was "Christian," and what was not?

VII

DRAMA AND THE DANCE

"A good play has no audience." What truth is there in such a statement?

Distinguish between tragedy and comedy. Does tragedy always bring death? Is comedy always funny?

What is it that makes a play Christian? Is it always possible to state whether a play is Christian or not? Can a gay comedy ever be called Christian?

What is it that makes a play suitable for production in church? Can a gay comedy ever be so classified?

Where do you think the line should be drawn between education and propaganda? Can propaganda ever be Christian? Can a play which seeks to propagandize (even for Christianity) be called good art?

In what sense is a service of church worship dramatic? Is there any difference here between the "Word of God" service and the "Upper Room" service?

What is the difference between being dramatic and being theatrical?

Does drama hold equal value for children, young people, and adults?

Why is it that the Roman Catholic Church, generally considered to be more "artistic" than Protestant groups, does not seem to be so much interested as the Protestants in the modern recovery of church drama?

Should a Christian church ever produce a Greek (pagan) play?

Should churches encourage their members and young people to write their own plays or depend largely upon the masters for their dramatic material?

Are medieval plays too romantic and naïve for us to seek to revive?

Has dancing ever a proper place in the church, or have recent efforts in this direction gone too far?

If dancing can ever be proper in church, what kind? Why is ballet dancing not deemed to be suitable? Why has the feeling against dancing in church persisted while that against music has not?

What are the emotional values in a service of lights? Intellectual values?

Should a church seek to organize a dramatic, dancing, or choral speaking group before it is convinced that it can do it well? Or should it plunge in and make a beginning with what resources it has available?

What is the value of realistic scene settings and costuming? What are the objections? Do the same arguments hold in church as in a theater?

Discuss the relative values of chancel and platform for church plays.

What hope do you hold out for drama in helping to revive worship in our churches?

VIII

PICTURES AND SCULPTURE

Is it true that painting is a more individualistic art than music, drama, and most of the others? Can a painting ever express the thoughts and emotions of a large and heterogeneous group?

What is greatness in painting and sculpture? Which is more important: greatness of soul or greatness of skill?

Have we Protestants been right in excluding pictures from our churches? Would Christianity have developed in a better way, as far as worship is concerned, if the Catholic Church had retained the old Jewish rule of no human representations? (Compare Christianity with Mohammedanism in this regard.)

What is it that makes a painting or statue Christian?

What do you look for in a picture of Jesus? Is there any painting that you know that fulfills your ideals?

What is the difference between idolatry and the use of "worship centers"?

If we encourage worship centers, with pictures of Jesus, why object to a crucifix with the carved figure of Jesus?

Is there the same objection to a crucifix bearing the risen Christ as there is to one with the dead Christ?

Why is it that many people are willing to sing about the cross (even such words as "Hold thou thy cross before my closing eyes") and yet object to the presence of a cross before their eyes in church? Is there a legitimate distinction here?

Do you think the Eastern rule of pictures but no statues a helpful compromise?

What is it that modern paintings—so strange to one accustomed to the "marvelous likeness!" style—are really trying to do?

Why is it that this so-called modernistic style, for so long scorned and repressed, is now sweeping almost everything before it?

Should we Protestants keep our churches open weekdays, more than we do, for private prayer, rest, and devotion? If so, what effect will this have on our interior arrangements and embellishments? What values are there, if any, in the Roman Catholic stations of the cross?

Should every single picture in the parish house be chosen with a view to its Christian expressiveness? What is the value in the "gallery of former pastors"?

What can we do to improve the art on church calendars, Sunday-school cards, wedding certificates, and the like?

Should every picture in a Christian home be chosen from a Christian viewpoint?

IX

THE ARTIST HIMSELF

Having come to the last chapter, check up now on the author's contention that art involves awareness of an object, relationship to it, and reaction.

Does reaction necessarily involve creativeness?

What accounts for taste? Even brothers brought up in the same home often have differences. Why? Can taste be changed? Should we ever try to change anyone's taste? Who shall judge as to the direction of such a proposed change?

How can we tell, fundamentally, whether a certain type of architecture, or picture, or piece of music, is "good" or "bad"?

Name ways other than those called "worship" in which we can express our reactions to God.

What is the nearest art museum to your home? Is it a good one? How do you know? With what proportion of its regularly exhibited objects are you familiar? Would it be a good Christian objective to take your Sunday-school class or other church group to become acquainted with these objects?

Have you visited all the interesting neighboring churches?

What opportunities for art education are there in your community? If there are not enough, what can you do to further the cause?

Discuss the plan put forth in this chapter for a local "Arts Guild" in your church. How many people do you think would respond? How would you go about establishing one? Would it be worth while?

What has artistic creativity to do with nervous states? With knowledge of history? With social and economic viewpoint? With occupational activity? With appreciation of nature? With family happiness? With general cultural life? With religious depth? With appreciation of Jesus?

Is the Church as an institution a work of art? If so, who are its creators? How much time is it worth to seek to be a fellow creator of the Church?

Is worship the most important act in which Christian people can ever possibly engage?

B

Some Books to Read

I

Tolstoi, Leo: *What Is Art?* Oxford, 1930.

Bell, Clive: *Art,* London, Chatto and Windus, 1924.

Maritain, Jacques: *Art and Scholasticism,* New York, Sheed and Ward, 1933.

Gill, Eric: *Beauty Looks after Herself,* New York, Sheed and Ward, 1933.

Cheney, Sheldon: *The Story of Modern Art,* New York, The Viking Press, 1941.

Vogt, Von Ogden, *Art and Religion,* New Haven, Yale, 1921.

Dearmer, Percy, *Art and Religion,* London, S.C.M., 1924.

Bailey, Conant, Smith and Eastman: *The Arts and Religion,* New York, Macmillan, 1944.

Bailey, Albert E.: *Art and Character,* New York, Abingdon, 1938.

II

Bradley, Dwight: *Creative Worship,* Boston, Pilgrim Press, 1931.

Sperry, Willard L.: *Reality in Worship,* New York, Macmillan, 1939.

Underhill, Evelyn: *Worship,* New York, Harper, 1937.

Brenner, Scott F.: *The Way of Worship*, New York, Macmillan, 1944.

Heiler, F.: *The Spirit of Worship*, London, 1926.

Hislop, D. H.: *Our Heritage in Public Worship*, Edinburgh, 1935.

Hardman, Oscar: *A History of Christian Worship*, Nashville, Cokesbury, 1937.

Maxwell, W. D.: *An Outline of Christian Worship*, Oxford, 1936; with excellent bibliography of service books for church worship.

Freeman, Elmer S.: *The Lord's Supper in Protestantism*, New York, Macmillan, 1945.

Vogt, Von Ogden, *Modern Worship*, New Haven, Yale, 1927.

Seidenspinner, Clarence: *Form and Freedom in Worship*, Chicago, Willett, 1941.

Zernov, Nicolas, *The Church of the Eastern Christians*, New York, Macmillan, 1942.

Dunney, Joseph A.: *The Mass*, New York, Macmillan, 1933.

III

Short, Ernest H.: *A History of Religious Architecture*, New York, Macmillan, 1936.

Hamilton, John A.: *Byzantine Architecture and Decoration*, New York, Scribner, 1934.

Conant, Kenneth J.: *A Brief Commentary on Medieval Church Architecture*, Baltimore, Johns Hopkins, 1942.

Cram, Ralph Adams: *The Substance of Gothic*, Boston, Marshall Jones, 1917.

Batsford and Fry: *The Cathedrals of England*, New York, Scribner, 1936.

Embury, Aymar II: *Early American Churches*, New York, Doubleday Page, 1914.

Fleming, Daniel J.: *Heritage of Beauty*, New York, Friendship Press, 1937.

Webber, F. R.: *The Small Church*, Cleveland, J. H. Jansen, 1939.

Scotford, John R.: *The Church Beautiful*, Boston, Pilgrim Press, 1945.

Cheney, Sheldon, *The New World Architecture*, New York, Longmans Green, 1930.

Saint and Hugh: *Stained Glass of the Middle Ages in England and France*, London, A. and C. Black, 1913.

Connick, Charles J.: *Adventures in Light and Color*, New York, Random House, 1937.

IV

Webber, F. R.: *Church Symbolism,* Cleveland, J. H. Jansen, 1927.

Goldsmith, Elizabeth E.: *Sacred Symbols in Art,* New York, Putnam, 1912.

Stafford, T. A.: *Christian Symbolism,* New York, Cokesbury, 1942.

Fleming, Daniel J.: *Christian Symbols in a World Community,* New York, Friendship Press, 1940.

Bevan, Edwyn R.: *Symbolism and Belief,* New York, Macmillan, 1938.

Sullivan, John F.: *The Visible Church,* New York, Kennedy, 1921.

Dearmer, Percy: *The Parson's Handbook,* Oxford, 1921.

Unwin, Francis S.: *Decorative Arts in the Service,* London, Mowbray, 1912.

Conroy, Ellen, *Symbolism of Colour,* London, Rider, 1921.

Cox and Harvey, *English Church Furniture,* London, 1908.

Gibson, George M.: *The Story of the Christian Year,* New York, Abingdon-Cokesbury, 1945.

V

Davies and Grace: *Music and Worship,* London, Eyre, 1935.

Ashton, Joseph W.: *Music in Worship,* Boston, Pilgrim Press, 1943.

Dickinson, E.: *Music in the History of the Western Church,* London, 1902.

Reese, Gustav: *Music in the Middle Ages,* New York, Norton.

Douglas, C. Winfred: *Church Music in History and Practice,* New York, Scribner, 1937.

Pratt, Waldo S.: *Musical Ministries in the Church,* New York, Revell, 1902.

Gardner and Nicholson: *Manual of English Church Music,* London, 1923.

Davison, Archibald D.: *Protestant Church Music in America,* New York, Schirmer, 1933.

Lightwood, J. T.: *Hymn Tunes and Their Story.* Epworth Press, 1923.

Dearmer, Percy: *Songs of Praise Discussed,* Oxford, 1933.

Wolfe, Dickinson and Dickinson: *The Choir Loft and Pulpit,* New York, H. W. Gray, 1943.

Hymns for Worship, New York, Association Press, 1939.

The Concord Anthem Books, ed. Davison and Foote, Boston, E. C. Schirmer.

A List of Phonograph Records for use with *Music in History,* by H. D. McKinney and W. R. Anderson, New York, American Book Co.

VI

Goodspeed, E. J.: *The Making of the English New Testament,* University of Chicago, 1925.

Price, Ira Maurice: *The Ancestry of Our English Bible,* New York, Harper, 1940.

Butterworth, Charles C.: *The Literary Lineage of the King James Bible, 1340–1611,* Philadelphia, University of Pennsylvania Press, 1941, with excellent bibliography.

Dearmer, Percy: *Everyman's History of the Prayer Book,* Milwaukee, Morehouse, 1931.

Buttrick, George Arthur: *Prayer,* Nashville, Abingdon-Cokesbury, 1942.

Steere, Douglas V.: *Prayer and Worship,* New York, Association Press, 1938, with good bibliography of devotional reading.

Oxford Book of English Mystical Verse, Oxford, 1917.

Benson, Louis F.: *The English Hymn,* New York, Doran, 1915.

Smith, F. Augustine: *Lyric Religion,* New York, Revell, 1931.

Foote, Henry Wilder: *Three Centuries of American Hymnody,* Cambridge, Harvard, 1940.

Britt, Matthew: *The Hymns of the Breviary and Missal,* New York, Benziger, 1922.

Pick, Bernhard: *Hymns and Poetry of the Eastern Church,* Eaton and Mains, 1908.

VII

Cheney, Sheldon: *The Theatre,* New York, Tudor, 1921.

O'Hara and Bro: *A Handbook of Drama,* Chicago, Willett Clark, 1938.

Ward, Winifred: *Creative Dramatics,* New York, Appleton, 1930.

Eastman and Wilson: *Drama in the Church,* New York, French, 1942.

Macgowan, Kenneth: *The Theatre of Tomorrow,* New York, 1921.

Alexander and Goslin: *Worship through Drama,* New York, Harper, 1930.

Bates, Katherine Lee: *The English Religious Drama,* Macmillan, 1913.

Young, Karl: *The Drama of the Medieval Church,* Oxford, 1933, 2 vols.

Osgood, Phillips Endecott: *Old Time Church Drama Adapted,* New York, Harper, 1928.

Harrison, Margaret H.: *Modern Religious Drama in Germany and France,* Boston, Stratford, 1936.

Bibliography of Plays, entitled *Religious Dramas* (3¢ each), Chicago Theological Seminary.

Simonson, Lee: *Part of a Lifetime,* New York, Duell, Sloan and Pearce, 1943.

VIII

Barnes, Albert C.: *The Art in Painting,* New York, 1928.

Faure, Elie: *History of Art* (4 vols.), trans. Pach, New York, Harper, 1921–24.

Morey, Charles R.: *Early Christian Art,* Princeton, 1942.

Morey, Charles R.: *Medieval Art,* New York, W. W. Norton, 1943.

Mâle: *The Religious Art of the Thirteenth Century in France,* trans. Nussey, New York, Dutton, 1913.

Coulton, G. G.: *Art and the Reformation,* New York, Knopf, 1928.

Cheney, Sheldon: *A Primer of Modern Art,* New York, Tudor, 1939.

Pearson, Ralph M.: *The New Art Education,* New York, Harper, 1941.

Fry and Binyon: *Chinese Art,* London, Batsford, 1925.

Fleming, Daniel J.: *Each with His Own Brush,* New York, Friendship Press, 1938.

Bailey, Albert E.: *The Gospel in Art,* Boston, Pilgrim Press, 1936.